The Jíbaro and the Gaucho United in Music and Song

Anthony L. Sánchez Cruz

All rights reserved.

The reproduction and public distribution of the contents of this book, for commercial purposes, in any format and with any support of technical media, without expressed authorization from the author, is strictly prohibited.

© 2018 (Original Spanish Version), 2019 Anthony L. Sanchez Cruz

English translation by Anthony L. Sanchez Cruz

Photography and Book Cover Design by Maria Goretti Cruz

978-0-9958485-3-5

The Jíbaro and the Gaucho
United in Music and Song

English Translation by Anthony L. Sánchez Cruz

Table of Contents

	Page
List of Tables	9
List of Examples	10
Introduction	11
About the English Edition of This Book	13
Folklore and Peculiar Phrases	15
How Foreigners Viewed the Jíbaro	18
Excerpt from *El gibaro: Cuadro de costumbres de la isla de Puerto-Rico*	18
Excerpt from *El campesino puertorriqueño: sus condiciones físicas, intelectuales y morales, causas que las determinan y medios para mejorarlas*	19
Characterizations of the Puerto Rican Jíbaro in the Nineteenth and Twentieth Century	21
Visualizations of the Gaucho in Literature and Music	27
Excerpt from *El Gaucho Martin Fierro* by José Hernández	31
Other Cultures in Puerto Rican and Argentine Folk Music	33
The Development of the Theory of Transculturation: 1940s-1980s	35

Table of Contents (Continued)

The Development of the Theory of Transculturation: 1980s-2010s 41

Technology of the Times 52

Radio in Puerto Rico and Argentina 52

Receivers 54

What Radio Listeners Waited For 55

The Governments and Radio Programming 56

Musical Recordings 59

A Transcultural Link with Technology 61

Origins and Structure of the Puerto Rican Seis 64

The Seis as a Dance 65

The Music of the Seis in Puerto Rico 69

Musical Pentagram 70

Musical Aspects of the Puerto Rican Seis: Analyses of Three Seis 72

Rhythm 73

Table of Contents (Continued)

New Musical Identity: Melodic and Harmonic Analyses of Three Types of Puerto Rican Seis 75

Seis Milonga 76

Seis Tango 77

Seis Pampero 78

The Tango Canción 80

The Décima: Reevaluating its Structure and Performance 82

The Origin and Structure of the Argentine Payada 86

Comparisons Between the Argentine Payada and the Puerto Rican Seis 88

Musical Instruments and Elements 90

Puerto Rican "Controversias" and Argentine "Contrapuntos" 91

Preserving the Art of Improvisation 92

Conclusion 95

<u>Appendix:</u>

Table of Puerto Rican and Argentine Folk Music 97

Table of Contents (Continued)

Works Cited
.... 97

Bibliography
.... 97

Webography
.... 102

Discography
.... 106

List of Tables

Table 1: Chronology and Comparison of Historical and Musical Events in Puerto Rico and Argentina: 1815-1945 45

Table 2: Investigations on the Theory of Transculturation 49

Table 3: Structure of the "Seis Milonga" 79

Table 4: Structure of the "Seis Tango" 79

Table 5: Structure of the "Seis Pampero" 79

Table 6: "Cambalache," Harmonic Analysis 81

Table 7: Concepts of Poetic Structure 83

Table 8: Stanza Forms 84

Table 9: General Structure of the Décima 85

Table 10: Examples of the Argentine Payada Puerto Rican Décima 88

Table 11: Rules for Rhymes in a Puerto Rican Décima 90

List of Examples:

Example 1: Habanera Rhythm ("café con pan")
.... 73

Example 2: Cinquillo Rhythm
.... 74

Example 3: "Cha-chiqui-cha" Rhythm
.... 74

"La cuestión no es llegar, sino quedarse."

("The question is not to arrive, but rather to stay.")

Introduction:

"We were not born with a book under our arms; we write our own oral history…" It is an affirmation of the history of the *jíbaro* (mountain man) and the *gaucho* (South American cowboy) in relation to the legendary folk music philosophy. Oral history is one of the most powerful tools encountered in almost every type of civilization. But, many times "the story of comrades" alters history depending on how news arrives. The music of the folk in Latin American and the Caribbean deserves reporting, documentation and study; in this way, one discovers the grand richness of these cultures.

The rural customs of the jíbaro and gaucho often parallel each other in their representations of everyday life. From a historical standpoint, these people have served as inspiration for poets, authors, musicians, and scholars among others. It does not matter whether they know the jíbaro and gaucho as *cantores, troveros, metristas, copleros, rimadores, trovadores,* or *payadores*. These names derive from similarities with the English troubadour from the Middle Ages. Scholars and music specialists comprehend that these names refer to the folkloric depictions of traditional music from regions of Spain, Argentina, Puerto Rico, and other parts of South America and the Caribbean. Through the decades, many have written innumerable books related to the gaucho and his music: as well as the jíbaro.

This book attempts to establish a transcultural link between the *música campestre (countryside music)* of Puerto Rican and Argentine folk music: innate folkloric and cultural elements inherited from Spain and Cuba. Referring to "cultural heritage," I include at the beginning of every section peculiar phrases and refrains which are gradually disappearing from linguistic use with each new generation. This study also compares the poetic and musical structures of the Puerto Rican *seis*, the Argentine *payada* and the *tango cancion* (tango song). In order to support the similar characteristics between Argentina and Puerto Rico, the book devotes time to exploring the different approaches to the theory of *transculturation*: how scholars define, expand upon and apply it. Additionally, the research presented here examines how anthropologists, writers and musicologists define the terms *folklore, peculiar phrases, tradition,* and *culture*.

One must also remember to view certain literature about the folk cultures from Puerto Rico and Argentina in terms of their historical significance to understand their cultural universality. It is these which, through poetry and peculiar phrases, enable readers to comprehend the playfulness, talent and patriotism of these countrymen and women. It becomes indispensable to graphically describe the history of the jíbaro and gaucho, one that also reflects the everyday life through the highs and lows of governments, outbreaks and natural disasters.

It is evident that new technologies and investigative processes from the twenty-first century can often replace previous fictional narratives and theories, where several scholars express personal opinions, while others apply concrete documentation. The following study attempts to present readers with complete and justifiable examples from different eras. It illustrates the effects of musical transculturation through devices likes wax cylinder recordings, phonographic discs and radio. When the technology of the times enabled listeners to instill a creative consciousness, it gave inspiration for new forms of Puerto Rican folk music. This occurred in the period from the 1900s until the 1940s, when cylinders, records and radio served as the primary forms of entertainment for the metropolitan and rural communities. To compare these points, this book includes a brief summary of the history of Puerto Rico and Argentina in the nineteenth and twentieth century.

This study includes sections involving the application of Western music theory in relation to the folk music from both countries. I present the analyses clearly and precisely, in basic formats with visual musical examples, tables with formulas, rules and structures. In the book, I demonstrate basic structural analyses of the Puerto Rican musical terms and genres involving improvisation like *décima*, seis and *controversia* (controversy) and explain the Argentine payada and *desafío* (challenge) or *contrapunto* (counterpoint) subgenre. Although these sections can prove complex for people who enjoy these types of music but are not trained in the musical field, it is necessary to demonstrate the formulas and components that constitute the analytical processes behind the music. Information in this study concerning the Argentine tango covers the early decades from the 1920s to 1940s: factors like the political impact on Argentine tango and how tango influenced Argentine society and culture, like "Cambalache": the tango song from the 1930s with pessimistic lyrics that can still apply to the present times.

This study also includes details about styles of the Puerto Rican seis inspired by the tango and other music from Argentina. As part of these sections, it also includes comparisons between the seis and Argentine payada. To graphically demonstrate these comparative analyses between the two cultures, it includes tables, citations of transcriptions, illustrations, and other necessary resources available to reveal the musical relation between these two regions of the world.

About the English Edition of This Book

The material presented in this current edition derives from my translation of the original Spanish version of the book, *El jíbaro y el gaucho unidos en música y cancion* (2018). I also perceive this book and the original Spanish version as a continuation and expansion of my work on the musical application of the theory of transculturation. I had previously discussed this theory in relation to Puerto Rican folk instruments from the perspective of music composition.[1]

Readers should not expect to encounter a literal English translation of the original Spanish in this book. I have also attempted to edit, expand or rephrase parts of the text which, if left in their original form, would demonstrate awkward moments or inconsistencies for readers not familiar the Spanish language and grammar. Where appropriate, I include English translations of specific block quotes or sections, followed by the same

---

[1] Anthony Luis Sanchez, *The Puerto Rican Cuatro as a Device for Transculturation: A Contemporary Compositional Approach in Estampas de La Isla del Encanto* (Athens, GA: University of Georgia), 2017 DMA Dissertation, http://dbs.galib.uga.edu/cgi-bin/getd.cgi?userid=galileo&serverno=22&instcode=publ (accessed November 27, 2018).

quote or section in the original Spanish language in parentheses. It also deserves mention at the outset of this book that some of the translations often detract from the linguistic effectiveness of the Spanish texts. For example, English translations of Spanish poetry excerpts in this book lose their original rhyme scheme. Other instances involve Spanish words or phrases that have no direct English equivalent, which results in forming educated guesses through translation.

When translating the Spanish poetry into English, I had to consider the application of Latin American and Caribbean dialects in the texts. Concerning Argentine folk culture, some of the poems featured in this book use the gaucho and *lunfardo* languages by combining Spanish and Italian. As I will discuss later in this study, the lunfardo dialect reflects the slang language used by European immigrants who moved to Argentina in the late nineteenth century. In the case of Puerto Rico, some poems intentionally apply the jíbaro slang by dropping consonants or vowels.

"Cuanto más se vive, más se aprende."

("The more you live, the more you learn.")

Folklore and Peculiar Phrases

Before establishing a relation among the terms *folklore*, *peculiar phrases*, *tradition*, and *culture*, it is common in the language from Latin American and Caribbean regions to use peculiar phrases or sayings. Concerning the term "peculiar phrases," Jorge Duany suggests that language carries light in the shadow of popular culture: positive elements of daily life and common expressions that explain picaresque situations and doses of humor.[2] As an example, for the Puerto Rican jíbaro (mountain man), a peculiar phrase consists of something like, "So clearly that a rooster can really sing" ("Más claro no canta un gallo."). This phrase refers to how the truth is as clear as the voice of a rooster. By contrast, the Argentine gaucho (rancher or cowboy) uses phrases like, "Happier than on the day that I have mate[3] with fried pie" ("Más alegre que día de mate con torta frita."). This refers to how they drink mate every day and some days have something extra to accompany the drink.

William Thoms of England first used the word *folklore* in 1846. In the Spanish language, it is acceptable to write this word in multiple ways as follows: *folklor, folclor* or *folklore*. This term is often defined as the mundane conditions of daily life and containing mythological and religious elements.[4] Some examples of this are the words "jíbaro" and "gaucho".

---

[2] Noticias: Locales: Frases peculiares de la cultura boricua ," *El nuevo día*, martes, el 26 de noviembre de 2013,
https://www.elnuevodia.com/noticias/locales/nota/frasespeculiaresdelaculturaboricua-1652910/ (accessed March 10, 2018).

[3] This word is pronounced, "ma-teh" and refers to a strong drink akin to coffee or tea.

[4] Jonathan Roper, "'Our National Folklore': William Thoms as Cultural Nationalist," in *Narrating the (Trans) Nation: The Dialects of Culture and Identity*, editada por Krishna Sen y Sudeshna Chakravari (Calcutta, ID: Das Gupta & Co., 2008), 60-74.
https://www.academia.edu/835266/_Our_National_Folklore_William_Thoms_as_Cultural_Nationalist (accessed March 10, 2018); Luis Manuel Álvarez, "La décima en Puerto Rico como símbolo de identidad nacional," Valledupar, CO: *Foro Internacional sobre la Décima*. 2001. Conference.

They do not necessarily refer to their etymology, if not to the sense of daily life.

It is imperative not to confuse folklore with *tradition*, which is a term with completely different connotations and implications. Tradition, according to Raúl Chuliver, stems from how people transmit beliefs, superstitions and news from generation to generation.[5] In the case of the Puerto Rican jíbaro, this refers to the oral tradition of singing décimas. The Argentine gaucho uses the oral tradition of singing payadas.

Culture proves more complicated in terms of locating a clear and concise definition. As will be discussed later in this study, not all scholars agree on this aspect. One possible definition derives from Edward B. Tylor, who perceives culture as a complete concept in that it involves acquiring knowledge and ideas through reading, study and work.[6]

Literature and poetry serve as other elements for expressing universality. Argentina applied Nationalism through the representation and preservation of Castilian Spanish and gaucho literature, like the poems by José Hernández (1834-1886) and Eduardo Gutiérrez (1851-1889). Around this same period, Puerto Rico still served as the last Spanish colony. The island produced authors like Manuel Alonso (1822-1889) and poets like Luis Llorens Torres (1876-1944) among others. To demonstrate the influence of gaucho poetry on the island of Puerto Rico, I feature the "Trova gaucha" ("Gaucho Ballad") by Llorens Torres:

> The Iberian Lion, which one day
> was the owner of the Pampa
> I orchestrated the trap
> that made it my prisoner.
> Saint Martin was my ultimate guide

---

http://musica.uprrp.edu/lalvarez/seiseshtm/decima.htm (accessed September 2, 2017).

[5] Raúl Chuliver, "El gaucho en la historia y en la tradición argentina," (Buenos Aires: Premio Santa Clara de Asís, 2015) *Biblioteca virtual Miguel de Cervantes*, http://www.cervantesvirtual.com/obra-visor/el-gaucho-en-la-historia-y-en-la-tradicion-argentina-784360/html/ (accessed March 10, 2018).

[6] Bruno Nettl, " 16: Music and 'That Complex Whole': Studying Music in or as Culture," in *The Study of Ethnomusiclogy: Thirty-Three Discussions* (Urbana, IL: Imprenta de La Universidad de Illinois, 2015), 231-247.

In that fertile gesture,
and neither roses, nor elegance,
nor the Devil who reared them,
(can) extinguish the sun that I
lit in the new world.

(Al ibero León que un día
era dueño de la Pampa
supe tenderle la trampa
que lo hizo presa mía.
Fue San Martin mi alto guía
en aquel gestí fecundo,
y ni Rosas, ni Facundo,
ni el diablo que los crio,
apagan el sol que yo
encendí en el nuevo mundo.)[7]

---

[7] Luis Llorens Torres, "Trova gaucha." *Proyecto salón de hogar*, el 19 de abril de 2010, http://www.proyectosalonhogar.com/escritores/Poesia_puertorriquena.htm#llorens (accessed March 10, 2018). This poem refers to Argentine geography via the plains (pampas) and alludes to the epic poem, "El gaucho Martin Fierro" by Jose Hernandez through "Saint Martin."

"La verdad, aunque severa, es amiga verdadera…"

("The truth, although severe, is the truest friend.")

How Foreigners Viewed the Jíbaro

Excerpt from *El gíbaro: Cuadro de costumbres de la isla de Puerto-Rico*

> Dark color, clear front.
>
> Medium size, moderately marching, the soul of illusions ahead   acute ingenuity, free and arrogant to think restlessly, hot-headed
>
> Human, affable, just, generous in the company of love always changing,
>
> Always industrious toward glory and pleasure.
>
> And inseparably in love with his land!
>
> This is, without a doubt, a faithful design to copy a good Puerto Rican.
>
> (Color moreno, frente despejada.
>
> Mediana talla, marcha compasada, el alma de ilusiones adelante agudo ingenio, libre y arrogante pensar inquieto, mente acalorada.
>
> Humano, afable, justo, dadivoso en empresa de amor siempre variable,
>
> tras la gloria y placer siempre afanoso.
>
> ¡Y en amor a su patria inseparable!
>
> Este es, año dudarlo fiel diseño para copia un buen puertorriqueño.) [8]

---

[8] Manuel Alonso, "Escena V. Bailes de Puerto-Rico," in *El gíbaro: Cuadro de costumbres de la isla de Puerto-Rico* (Barcelona: D. Juan Oliveres, 1849) 55-68 (accessed April 14, 2015). Public Domain.

The Jíbaro and the Gaucho

Excerpt from *El campesino puertorriqueño: sus condiciones físicas, intelectuales y morales, causas que las determinan y medios para mejorarlas.*

The following historical excerpt from Fransisco del Valle Atiles does not reflect my opinions as an author. I have presented my translation of this section (followed by the original Spanish text) as a detailed visualization of how *other* people perceived the Puerto Rican jíbaros in the past. Notice in the description of the facial features for jíbaro men and women that Valle Atiles praises *meztisaje*, or cultural mixing between the African and European people. He also wastes no time in expressing ethnocentric ideas and vitriolic criticism about what he perceives as the "ugliness" of African faces.

Cranium and Face—The cranium of the jíbaro does not offer any deformities. The face presents agreeable traits; the eyes are big, lively and are horizontally situated; in rare instances on can encounter oblique eyes like the Chinese; the nose is well-formed and the mouth small.
Among the women, these traits are greatly and delicately acquired; among all of these, the beauty of the black eyes is common among them.

These facial attributes change for the countryman descended from the Africans, in which the nose is wide and the thick lips deform the mouth, large in general.

Among the meztisos one encounters people not exempt from beauty, which is maximized when the predominantly Caucasian element is instilled in them; among all of these the women are lovely, but for the men the nose and mouth of African elements are transmitted to the mestizo with their characteristic form and ruining their factions.

(*Cráneo y cara*—El cráneo del jíbaro no ofrece deformidad alguna. La cara presenta rasgos agradables; los ojos son grandes, vivos y están horizontalmente situados; por rareza se encuentran ojos oblicuos como los de los chinos; la nariz es bien formada y la boca pequeña.

Entre las mujeres estos rasgos adquieren mayor delicadeza; sobre todo la hermosura de los ojos negros es común entre ellas.

Estos rasgos fisonómicos cambian en el campesino descendiente de africanos, en el cual la nariz es ancha y los labios son gruesos deformando la boca, grande por lo general.

Entre los mestizos se encuentran personas no exentas de hermosura, máxime cuando en ellas predomina el elemento caucásico; sobre todo entre las mujeres las hay bellas, pero por lo general la nariz y la boca del elemento africano se trasmiten al mestizo con sus formas características afeando las facciones.) [9]

---

[9] Francisco del Valle Atiles, *El campesino puertorriqueño: sus condiciones físicas, intelectuales y morales, causas que las determinan y medios para mejorarlas.* (San Juan: Tipo de Gonzales Font, 1889), 12, https://freeditorial.com/es/books/el-campesino-puertorriqueno-sus-condiciones-fisicas-intelectuales-y-morales (accessed February 4, 2018), Public Domain.

"El que no oye consejos, no llega a viejo."

("He who does not hear advice does not grow old.")

Characterizations of the Puerto Rican Jíbaro in the Nineteenth and Twentieth Century

Referring to Bruno Nettl (b. 1930) in his essays about ethnomusicology and considering that ethnomusicology attempts to apply the concept of music from the perspective of the society under investigation, it can nonetheless demonstrate moments of ethnocentric biases. Nettl suggests that, despite a desire for impartiality in representing foreign cultures, it remains inevitable that ethnomusicologists will commit these mistakes.[10] Even though Nettl writes from an ethnomusicological perspective, concentrating on ethnocentric tendencies and ambiguities, the same information can apply to the discoveries uncovered in this current study. I attempt to fairly represent Puerto Rican and Argentine cultures. However, I also cannot ignore the sociocultural effects of the Spanish European and other foreign influences on these Latin American and Caribbean regions. First, one must focus on how these dominant cultures tried to marginalize, alter or erase the historical and cultural value from these areas of the world. Sometimes, these processes and effects would involve applying Nationalism in literature and music in the nineteenth and twentieth century.

Based on investigations and documented materials dating from the United States occupation of Puerto Rico (1898-1952), like scientific and ethnographic studies, it becomes clear that foreign scholars at that time took notice of the jíbaro culture. John Alden Mason is best remembered and frequently cited for his efforts in compiling and cataloging Puerto Rican folk music in 1918.[11] Whereas Mason discusses

---

[10] Bruno Nettl, "2: Combining Tones: On the Concept of Music," in *The Study of Ethnomusiclogy: Thirty-Three Discussions* (Urbana, IL: University of Illinois Press, 2015), 29.

[11] J. Alden Mason and Aurelio M. Espinosa. "Puerto Rican Folklore. Décimas, Christmas Carols, Nursery Rhymes, and Other Songs," Diario del 31, No. 121 (1918), http://www.jstor.org/stable/534783, (accessed January 19, 2018).

this music and Puerto Rican folk culture from a mostly positive perspective, other early twentieth-century studies from the United States do not share such enthusiasm: choosing, instead, to employ scientific racism and ethnocentrism. William H. Hass clearly demonstrates moments of racial prejudice in his 1936 study about the Puerto Rican jíbaro. Haas concentrates on what he perceives as the regressive social and intellectual nature of the jíbaro, at times equating him through stereotyping to rural United States southerners. Based on his perverse logic, Haas suggests that the jíbaro stubbornly rejects modernization and refuses to acknowledge his US citizenship.[12]

In many cases, the negative portrayal that Haas presents in his study on jíbaro culture from the US perspective in the 1930s mirrors similar Spanish European sentiments from the nineteenth century. Many Puerto Rican historians and musicologists frequently refer to (and overuse) the 1849 book *El gíbaro: cuadro de costumbres de la isla de Puerto-Rico* (*The Gíbaro: Pictures of Customs from the Island of Puerto Rico*), written by the Spanish Creole author Manuel Alonso (1822-1889). One reason for the excessive citation of this book stems from how Alonso describes the Puerto Rican *cuatro* and other types of musical instruments and dances from the island.[13] However, readers should not assume that an archaic source like *El gíbaro* contains accurate information merely because it dates from an older century. Investigating this book from a more contemporary perspective, one can notice the tendency for Manuel Alonso to present a romanticized version of Puerto Rican rural life. Alonso does not present facts. Instead, he devotes most of his book to expressing negative depictions and personal opinions about jíbaro culture compared to the aristocratic European Spanish lifestyle. In addition to these problems, *El gíbaro* presents another critical obstacle because of its

---

[12] William H. Haas, "The Jíbaro: An American Citizen," *Scientific Monthly* 43, No. 1 (1936). http://www.jstor.org/stable/16218 (accessed June 6, 2016).

[13] Manuel Alonso, "Escena V. Bailes de Puerto-Rico," in *El gíbaro: Cuadro de costumbres de la isla de Puerto-Rico* (Barcelona: D. Juan Oliveres, 1849) 55-68, (accessed April 14, 2015), Public Domain.

frequent misuse as an authoritative source of information about Puerto Rican music and society.[14]

Contemporary research in the twenty-first century, like the book *Cuerdas de mi tierra* (*Strings from My Land*) from 2013, also recognizes the problems associated with *El gíbaro*. While most scholars now view that book as an archaic study, they still use it as historical reference material because of how people from the nineteenth century describe Puerto Rican music and dance.[15] Other historians, like Francisco A. Scarano and Carmen L. Torres-Robles conclude in their respective studies on colonial Puerto Rican history that Manuel Alonso concentrates more on expressing his personal interests and opinions than on concrete data. Scarano y Torres-Robles mention that Alonso presents Puerto Rican jíbaros in negative and degrading caricatures from the perspective of the Spanish aristocracy. Considering this point, he prefers to stereotype jíbaro society instead of trying to understand it: an aspect reflected in his application of dialectical writing. By candidly mocking Puerto Rican folk culture, Alonso does not demonstrate aspects of the real jíbaro people.[16] Given these points, modern readers of *El gíbaro* must avoid interpreting the book as a primary source about Puerto Rican history and culture.

Similar problems manifest themselves in the 1889 ethnographic study *El campesino puertorriqueño: sus condiciones físicas, intelectuales y morales, causas que las determinan y medios para mejorarlas* (*The Puerto Rican Mountain Man: His Physical Conditions, Intellect and Morals, Determining Causes, and Methods for Improving Them*) by Francisco Hilarión Del Valle Atiles (1852-1928). Valle Atiles describes the jíbaro community, the physical appearances of the people and (in certain instances) information related to musical

---

[14] Manuel Alonso, 55-68.

[15] Juan Sotomayor Pérez, William Cumpiano and Myriam Fuentes, "1. Inicio de la Jornada," en *Cuerdas de mi tierra: Una historia de los instrumentos de cuerda nativos de Puerto Rico: cuatro, tiple, vihuela y bordonúa* (Naguabo, PR: Extreme Graphics, 2013), 17-36.

[16] Francisco A. Scarano, "La mascarada del jíbaro y las políticas subalternas de la formación de la identidad criolla en Puerto Rico, 1745-1823," *Revista histórica americana* 101, No. 5 (1996), 1398-1431. http://jstor.org/stable/2170177 (accessed June 6, 2016); Carmen L. Torres-Robles, "La mitificación y desmitificación del jíbaro como símbolo de la identidad nacional puertorriqueña." *Bilingual Review/Revista Bilingüe* 24, No. 3, (1999), 241-153. http://www.jstor.org/stable/25745665 (accessed June 6, 2016).

instruments and dance. Throughout the book, he exhibits a racist tone in his descriptions: writing from the perspective of the medical science practices of his time. Like Manuel Alonso, Valle Atiles also concentrates on how he perceives rural Puerto Rican people and customs in the 1880s as "backwards" when compared to the European Spanish. Concerning musical instruments, he says the following:

> Let us talk, albeit briefly, about the musical instruments from the rural areas: the *maraca*, a species of sound of Indian origin, which by its name and sound produced, could be compared to a rattle, rough and a primitive representation of instruments from almost all uncivilized lands; the gourd (güiro), a bleak instrument for the ears not accustomed to the dry and messy sound produced by scraping its lined surface; and several derivations of the guitar and bandurria, which particularly deserve some consideration. There are these derivations: the *tiple*, guitarrillo with five strings, which present the inexplicable particularity of having the first and fifth string equal, which gives way to an anomalous combination of sounds; the *cuatro*, which has five doubled strings, placed two by two, is arranged like the bandurria and performed like that; the *bordonúa* contains six strings, and the *vihuela* up to ten, which brings the constructor (of musical instruments) joy…

> (Digamos algo, aunque brevemente, acerca de los instrumentos musicales campestres: la *maraca*, especie de sonaja de orígen indio, que por su nombre y por el ruido que produce, podría compararse con la matraca, tosco y primitivo representante del instrumental de casi todos los pueblos no civilizados; el güiro, desapacible instrumento para oídos no acostumbrados al guachapeo seco que ocasiona el raspear sobre su lineada superficie; y algunas derivaciones de la guitarra y de la bandurria, es cuanto en el particular se ofrece á nuestra consideración. Son estas derivaciones: el *tiple*, guitarrillo de cinco cuerdas, que ofrece la inexplicable particularidad de tener la prima y la quinta iguales, lo que dá lugar á una combinación anómala de sonidos; el *cuatro*, que tiene cinco cuerdas dobles, colocadas de dos en dos, se templa como la bandurria y se toca como esta; la *bordonúa* lleva seis cuerdas, y

la *vihuela* hasta diez, pues en esto entra por mucho el capricho del constructor…)[17]

Based on this description, notice the candid racism and animosity that the Spanish would express toward the rural inhabitants of Puerto Rico. Valle Atiles demonstrates a negative attitude about the construction of the musical instruments. Concerning the construction of chordophone (string) instruments, he concentrates on what he interprets as the poor instrument quality compared to the Spanish string instruments. From a more contemporary viewpoint, the alterations of the instruments that Valle Atiles discusses involve transculturation. Combining the practices of creating European and Latin American instruments, as Valle Atiles describes, the artisans and luthiers from the rural areas of Puerto Rico introduced new material to add to their culture:

> … None of these instruments follow a rational artistic idea in their construction; the little material value of these created instruments except for the same jíbaros who make them, who most of the time use the least helpful or appropriate tools. It would be interesting to see the process of deviation in this province behind making national Spanish string instruments; in these subsist the idea that presides over the construction of the guitars and bandurrias; but the belief that the tools used to make these instruments similar to the models that the Metropolis brought to the Spanish, this was because of their imperfect influence…
>
> (… Ninguno de estos instrumentos obedece en su construcción á una idea artística racional; el poco valor material de ellos hace que sólo los construyan los mismos jíbaros, quienes la mayor parte de las veces se valen de útiles poco apropiados. Sería interesante

---

[17] Francisco del Valle Atiles, *El campesino puertorriqueño: sus condiciones físicas, intelectuales y morales, causas que las determinan y medios para mejorarlas.* (San Juan: Tipo de Gonzales Font, 1889), 70, https://freeditorial.com/es/books/el-campesino-puertorriqueno-sus-condiciones-fisicas-intelectuales-y-morales (accessed February 4, 2018), Public Domain.

señalar el proceso de desviación que en esta provincia han seguido los citados instrumentos nacionales de cuerda; en ellos subsiste la

idea que preside á la construcción de guitarras y bandurrias; pero la carencia de utensilios para fabricarlos iguales á los modelos que de la Metrópoli trajeron los españoles, ha debido influir en la imperfección de aquellos…)[18]

As can be deduced from this quote, each person has his or her own opinion. Even though the descriptions shown here present negative attributes, opinions and assumptions, they demonstrate how a dominant culture can gradually transform over time. The decision to accept or reject this change depends upon the attitude of the oppressing culture.

---

[18] Francisco del Valle Atiles, 1889.

"No me fío del padrillo que ve la yegua y no relincha."

("I do not judge the stallion that looks at a mare and does not neigh.")

Visualizations of the Gaucho in Literature and Music

"A symbol of the pampas and true man, generous warrior, loving, courageous, savage gaucho, to say the best. Clothing loose in the wind, protagonist of a victorious story." —Ricardo Güiraldes

("Símbolo pampeano y hombre verdadero, generoso guerrero, amor, coraje, ¡salvaje! gaucho, por decir mejor. Ropaje suelto de viento, protagonista de un cuento vencedor.")—Ricardo Güiraldes

According to an investigation by Raúl Chuliver concerning historical aspects of Argentine gaucho culture, the gaucho lived a nomadic life. He lived in times of peace, until war pointed him to another destiny. Then, sitting firmly on his horse, he left his family to run close to the leader (of the group of comrades).[19] Whereas foreigners frequently view the Puerto Rican jibaro in disparaging terms (eg., uneducated, but dedicated to work and music), Argentine authors, poets and in certain cases classical music composers in the nineteenth and twentieth century observe the gaucho in a more positive light. They portray a romanticized version of the rustic South American rancher, and this vision often serves as a national symbol in Argentina, Uruguay, Paraguay, and Chile. The rugged personality of the gaucho frequently manifests itself in literary works, like the epic poem *El Gaucho Martín Fierro* (*The Gaucho Martin Fierro*) from 1872 and the novela *Juan Moreira* (1879-1880) by Euardo Gutierrez.[20] Other authors, like Leopoldo Lugones in his book *El payador* (*The Payador*) from 1916, attempts

---

[19] Raúl Chuliver, "El gaucho en la historia y en la tradición argentina," (Buenos Aires: Premio Santa Clara de Asis, 2015) *Biblioteca virtual Miguel de Cervantes*, http://www.cervantesvirtual.com/obra-visor/el-gaucho-en-la-historia-y-en-la-tradicion-argentina-784360/html/ (accessed March 10, 2018).

[20] José Hernández, *El gaucho Martín Fierro* (Buenos Aires, Imprenta de La Pampa, 1872), https://freeditorial.com/es/books/el-gaucho-martin-fierro (accessed February

to unite the legacy of the gaucho: specifically, the gaucho as "payador" with Argentine nationalism through the Greco-Latin heritage.[21]

A true sense of admiration for the legacy of the gaucho manifests itself in relation to the gaucho music of Argentina and music inspired by gaucho culture: preserving the payadas through *desafíos, contrapuntos* and other competitions involving poetic improvisation between two people. Historians frequently refer to the first published and documented desafio from 1894, where the Afro-Argentine Gabino Ezeiza competed and won against Pablo Vázquez.[22] It also deserves mention that, in the early years of the 1900s, Ezeiza recorded songs on wax cylinders. Awhile after his death in 1916, his legacy became etched in history when the duo of Antonio Bassi (composer) y Manuel Romero (lyricist) created a tribute to Ezeiza with their tango canción, *El adiós de Gabino Ezeiza* (*Goodbye, Gabino Ezeiza*).[23]

Gaucho music culture also appears in Latin American classical music from the twentieth century. The composer Alberto Ginastera (1916-1983), best remembered for his contributions to Argentine Nationalism and Modernism, wrote the gaucho ballet *Estancia,* Opus 8 in 1941. Years later, he created a condensed version as an orchestral suite. In both works, Ginastera attempts to capture the atmosphere of daily life for the gaucho, the hard work on the haciendas (estates) and the *malambo* dance competition among other gauchos.[24]

12, 2018), Public Domain; Historiador Argentino, *Argentina: cultura gaucha*, https://www.youtube.com/watch?v=eESgmILx4Y4&list=LL8mqJY4bOeb4IP285vKj4OA&index=3&t=0s (accessed February 8, 2018).

[21] Leopoldo Lugones, *El payador: Hijo de la Pampa (Tomo Primero)* (Buenos Aires: Otero & Co., 1916), http://letras.edu.ar/elpayador.pdf (accessed February 12, 2018), Public Domain.

[22] Matías N. Isolabella, "Estructuras de improvisación en la payada rioplatense: definición y análisis." Revista Argentina de Musicología 12-13 (2012). 151-182.

[23] Gabino Ezeiza, "Gabino Ezeiza & Guitarra- El Tango Patagones- 1905." https://www.youtube.com/watch?v=dOchX98rVnY&index=1&list=LL8mqlY4bOeb4IP285vKj4OA&t=0s (accessed February 8, 2018); Antonio De Bassi y Manuel Romero, "Ignacio Corsini- El adiós de Gabino Ezeiza- Milonga," https://www.youtube.com/watch?v=scIMM3TW8E0 (accessed February 8, 2018).

[24] Luis Gaeta (Narrador) y La Orquesta Sinfónica de Londres (Gisele Ben-Dor), *Ginastera: Estancia- Panambí* (Naxos, 2006), 21-29, Spotify.

Some readers might question why Argentina pays so much attention to the gauchos. Part of this stems from stylized perception of gaucho culture. Decades after the Argentine Government created a Constitution in 1853, the politicians began promoting Nationalism for the country. According to the revisions of that Constitution, they did not include the municipality of Bueno Aires as part of the country until 1859.[25] They used a nationalist model as one designed to teach and control the population of Argentina, promoting the Spanish Castilian language. Additionally, they stressed the importance of creole culture through literature pertaining to the gauchos. In certain cases, some Argentine authors applied gaucho literature to protest the reconstruction of their country by European immigration in the 1870s and 1880s, or to lament the decline of the gaucho culture towards the end of the nineteenth century. José Hernández addressed such themes in the epic poem *La vuelta de Martin Fierro (The Return of Martin Fierro)* from 1879.[26]

According to Raúl Chuliver, people first applied the term "gaucho" around the 1700s. It is important to momentarily separate the perception of the gaucho in aspects of poetry, music and literature as forms of entertainment with the true gaucho from actual history. The gaucho played a significant role in the militia in the 1810s. In that decade, Argentina fought for its independence against the Spanish Monarchy. It was at that time that Argentines began to view gauchos as representations of patriots loyal to their country. Chuliver explains that:

> When General José San Martín sent an informant to the Northern Army in 1814 who communicated that "the lone gauchos of Salta, are forming a resource war so terrible that they are obligated to detach a division whose sole objective is to extract mules and win," the supreme director of the United Provinces, Gervasio Posadas, ordered that the publication of this part in the porteño (Argentine) newspaper *The Gazette* omit the word gaucho, replacing it with patriotic countrymen. In this way, they incorporated this new

---

[25] *Constitución de la Nación Argentina Completa con los Tratados de Jerarqui Constitucional* (Buenos Aires: Biblioteca Virtual Universal, 2017), http://www.biblioteca.org.ar/libros/201250.pdf (accessed February 12, 2018).

[26] Historiador Argentino, *Argentina: cultura gaucha*, https://www.youtube.com/watch?v=eESgmILx4Y4&list=LL8mqJY4bOeb4IP285vKj4OA&index=3&t=0s (accessed February 8, 2018).

element in the nascent patriotism for a long time, the gaucho horsemen who for years provided an influential role in all wars. Because of this, one author wrote that patriotism was created on horseback. The horse and his rider served as two inseparable pieces: in time of peace in work and in times of war. No one can imagine the gaucho without his horse.

(Cuando el general José San Martín envió desde el Ejército del Norte en 1814 un informe donde comunicaba que «los gauchos de Salta solos, están haciendo al enemigo una guerra de recursos tan terrible que lo han obligado a desprender una división con el solo objeto de extraer mulas y ganado», el director supremo de las Provincias Unidas, Gervasio Posadas, ordenó que en la publicación de ese parte en el periódico porteño La Gaceta se omitiese la palabra gaucho, reemplazándola por el de patriotas campesinos. Así, se incorporaba para mucho tiempo aquel nuevo elemento en la patria naciente, la caballería gaucha que durante años tendría papel preponderante en todas las guerras. Por eso, un escritor dijo que la patria se había hecho a caballo. Caballo y jinete fueron dos piezas inseparables: durante la paz en el trabajo y durante la guerra. No se concibe el gaucho sin el caballo.)[27]

Chuliver does not mention the citation in his article. The information that he includes in that section of his research stems from the Argentine newspaper *La Gaceta* (1810-1821). The objective behind this newspaper aimed to publish articles concerning governmental acts of the first meeting. Its motto was "The times of happiness are those when one is obligated to feel and say what they want" (from the Roman historian Corelius Tácitus).

---

[27] Raul Chuliver, "El gaucho en la historia y en la tradición argentina," (Buenos Aires: Premio Santa Clara de Asís, 2015) *Biblioteca virtual Miguel de Cervantes*, http://www.cervantesvirtual.com/obra-visor/el-gaucho-en-la-historia-y-en-la-tradicion-argentina-784360/html/ (accessed March 10, 2018).

The Jíbaro and the Gaucho

Excerpt from *El Gaucho Martin Fierro* by José Hernández[28]

Here I begin to sing
To the tune of the vihuela
That the man whose extraordinary sorrow
Makes him lose sleep
As the solitary bird
Is consoled with song.

I ask all the saints in Heaven
To help me my thoughts
I ask them in this moment
In which I am going to sing my story
That they refresh my memory
And clear my understanding.

Come miraculous saints,
Come all to my aid,
That my tongue goes tied
And my vision confused;
I ask God to assist me
On such a rude occasion.

I have seen many singers,
With fame they have obtained,

---

[28] José Hernández, "I - Cantor y Gaucho," en *El gaucho Martin Fierro* (Buenos Aires, Imprenta de La Pampa, 1872), https://freeditorial.com/es/books/el-gaucho-martin-fierro (acceso el 12 de febrero de 2018), Public Domain.

And after the acquisition
They do not wish to sustain
It seems that without elaboration
They grow tired in their endeavors.

(Aquí me pongo a cantar
Al compás de la vigüela,
Que el hombre que lo desvela

Una pena estraordinaria
Como la ave solitaria
Con el cantar se consuela.

Pido a los Santos del Cielo
Que ayuden mi pensamiento;
Les pido en este momento
Que voy a cantar mi historia
Me refresquen la memoria
Y aclaren mi entendimiento.

Vengan Santos milagrosos,
Vengan todos en mi ayuda,
Que la lengua se me añuda
Y se me turba la vista;
Pido a Dios que me asista
En una ocasión tan ruda.

Yo he visto muchos cantores,
Con famas bien obtenidas,
Y que después de adquiridas
No las quieren sustentar
Parece que sin largar
se cansaron en partidas.)

"No son todos los que están, ni están todos los que son."
("It is not everyone who is here, nor is everyone who is supposed to be here.")

Other Cultures in Puerto Rican and Argentine Folk Music

To understand the origins of Puerto Rican and Argentine folk music in relation to the *seis*, música campera (countryside music) and the tango, it is important to recognize that other foreign cultures helped to form and disseminate these musical styles: particularly, the regions from Africa, Spain and Cuba. Many musicologists and historians have encountered confusing situations regarding how to properly catalog these types of music. One specific case involves definitions of the words *Milonga* and *Tango* in the nineteenth century.

In studies compiled from the 1970s to the present, defense of African culture serves as a significant component of Latin American and Caribbean music.[29] Puerto Rico has inherited the genres of the *bomba* and *plena*, while Argentina has inherited the *camdombe* and the lexicological origins of the musical terms *tango, payada* and *milonga*. Milonga comes from the African word *Quimbunda* and refers to the plural form of *mulonga* (meaning "word") Afro-Argentines applied the term milonga as a reference to the payadas and contrapuntos performed by the gauchos from the pampas and southern regions of the country, because the gauchos would sing their words.[30] In this case, it is important to understand that the milonga from the nineteenth century refers to the milonga campera and not the dance of the same name.

Concerning the tango, one should take into consideration that European immigrants were not the only people who contributed to this music. Also, one must recognize an Afro-Argentine connection. Contemporary sources explain that the etymology of the word "tango" had different connotations in Latin American colonial times. In his investigation on the tango, Héctor Benedetti indicates that this word in the 1830s did not refer to any dance, nor to the accompanying music. In actuality, the tango in that time period referred to a communal site only for Afro-Argentines. As he explains in his book, *Nueva historia del tango: De los*

---

[29] Alejandro Frigerio, "El Candombe Argentino: Crónica de una muerte anunciada," *Revista de Investigaciones Folklóricas* No. 8 (1993), 50-60.

[30] Very Tango Store, "La historia de la milonga," https://www.verytangostore.com/tango-milonga.html (accessed February 12, 2018).

orígenes al siglo XXI (*New History of the Tango: From Its Origins to the Twenty-First Century*), Benedetti says that blacks would convene at "tangos" to develop rituals and practices, used solely by their community.[31]

In many respects, the discrimination against European immigrants in the 1880s until the early decades of the twentieth century in Argentina parallels many situations in other countries. Perhaps a more problematic situation stemmed from the Argentine perception of Nationalism, which partially ignored the African influences, culture and music on the South American country.[32] Until the end of the 1960s, a multitude of sources and scholarly information suggested that the Afro-Argentine population "died out" or "disappeared" at the close of the nineteenth century. The logic used by historians in the past indicates that the population of Argentina became gradually replaced by the white European population. Ethnographic studies from the 1970s to the present times, however, attempt to demystify and correct this false information about Afro-Argentines. With new details and documentation from the 2000s and 2010s, Argentine historians have gradually come to the realization of the existence of this group of people neglected by the past.[33]

What about the Spanish and Cuban connections in relation to the music of Puerto Rico and Argentina? To answer this question, one must understand that the Spanish and Cuban culture form and provide the bases for musical and poetic structures. However, the information presented in this study will serve to refute or reconsider several concepts which, until recently, have been accepted as true: especially regarding the Spanish décima, its poetic structure and connections with Puerto Rico and Argentina.

---

[31] Héctor Benedetti, "1: De cuando el tango aún no era. En busca de sus primeras manifestaciones," en *Nueva historia del tango: De los orígenes al siglo XXI* (Buenos Aires: Siglo XXI Editores, 2016), 19.

[32] Alejandro Frigerio, "El Candombe Argentino: Crónica de una muerte anunciada," *Revista de Investigaciones Folklóricas* No. 8 (1993), 50-60.

[33] Sylvain B. Pooson, "*Entre Tango y Payada*: The Expression of Blacks in Argentina in the Nineteenth Century," *Confluencia* 20, No. 1 (2004), 87-99; "HD Programa 017- Temporada 8- Afroargentinos," https://www.youtube.com/watch?v=eUik0wa96HY&list=LL8mqJY4bOeb4IP285vKj4OA&index=2 (accessed February 8, 2018).

"Mas claro no canta un gallo."
("So clearly that a rooster can really sing.")

The Development of the Theory of Transculturation: 1940s-1980s

In recent investigations, many scholars have discovered that the theory of transculturation carries distinct global connotations in Latin America and other regions of the world. Criticisms concerning this theory have gradually expanded in the twentieth and twenty-first century. From the 1940s to 1980s, three scholars from Latin America and the Caribbean (Fernando Ortiz of Cuba, José Maria Arguedas of Peru and Ángel Rama of Uruguay) served to define transculturation as clearly as possible.

Information that I present in this section will concentrate primarily on how Ortiz, Arguedas and Rama explain and apply transculturation from sociological and literary perspectives. Additionally, it will examine how these details can relate to the rural culture in Puerto Rico and gaucho culture in Argentina. I also provide critical commentary focusing on the positive and negative aspects of transculturation, as well as explore some of the other research on this theory from the twentieth and twenty-first centuries. In discussing this topic, I will demonstrate that academic studies concerning musical transculturation—while extant—do not receive as much attention as they should.

Fernando Ortiz (1881-1969) defines transculturation for the first time in his 1940 book, *Contrapunto cubano, Tabaco y azúcar (Cuban Counterpoint, Tobacco and Sugar)*. In the second section of this work, Ortiz uses his theory to demonstrate what he perceives as a better alternative to the older theory of *acculturation*. Ortiz discusses the application and overuse of acculturation in relation to anthropological research from the 1930s, clarifying the differences between the two concepts. For Ortiz, acculturation involves the process of physically and socially transitioning from one culture to another.[34] Based on his description, acculturation concentrates primarily on acquiring a new culture while at the same time losing another.

To understand the importance of transculturation from Ortiz, one must first look at the problems presented by the older theory of

---

[34] Fernando Ortiz. "II. La etnografía y transculturación del Tabaco de Habana y los inicios de azúcar en América. 2: El fenómeno social de la transculturación y su importancia," en *Contrapunto cubano, Tabaco y azúcar* (Durham, NC: Duke University Press, 1940, 1995). 97-103.

acculturation from scholars like Margaret J. Kartomi. Kartomi rejects the concept of acculturation in her 1981 study on what she calls "cultural contact" and provides four reasons as to why acculturation does not work, writing from the perspective of the 1980s.[35] The first problem that Kartomi addresses in her research stems from applying and appropriating music from other cultures, such as obtaining foreign music from another hemisphere and applying it to the Western Hemisphere (eg., Europe and the United States). Acculturation in music contains a plethora of ethnocentric aspects because of the perception of foreign music as "exotic." In her research from her 1981 study, Kartomi doubts that a culture can exist in complete isolation. She also suggests the possibility that music combines more than one culture. Given this possibility, she sees no need to explain or establish connections between cultures that undergo the process of acculturation.[36]

The second problem that Kartomi encounters with the theoretical model of acculturation stems from the overall definition of the concept and how she demonstrates how other scholars interpret the theory in distinct ways. She investigates and addresses the history and lexicological problems with "culture" from the 1880s. Kartomi cites works from anthropologists Ralph Linton and Melville J. Herskvits because they both arrive at the conclusion that the term contains contradictions. Kartomi goes farther in her investigation and examines the complexities of the word "acculturate" to demonstrate that it signifies different meanings, like adapting to a culture, while another definition focuses on losing a culture.[37]

As a third point, Margaret J. Kartomi mentions that acculturation promotes aspects of racism. She refers to Fernando Ortiz in her research and the fact that Ortiz also views acculturation in negative terms. However, Kartomi neglects to indicate that Ortiz commits the same errors with his theory of transculturation. By focusing his writing on cultural differences, at times one can sense the presence of racist rhetoric. Kartomi indicates that the first application of acculturation occurred in the Spanish colonial times. She suggests that it proved neither beneficial nor wise for Europeans

---

[35] Margaret J. Kartomi, "The Processes and Results of Musical Culture Contact: A Discussion of Terminology and Concepts," *Ethnomusicology* 25, No. 2 (1981), 227-249, http://www.jstor.org/stable/851273 (accessed July 20, 2016).

[36] Margaret J. Kartomi, 1981.

[37] Margaret J. Kartomi, 1981.

to study indigenous and non-Western cultures while simultaneously conquering them through subjugation and Christian proselytization. In committing these acts (and attempting to educate other Europeans about foreign cultures through printed documentation), European settlers and missionaries promoted ethnocentric ideals of their cultural "superiority" over the "inferiority" of non-Western foreigners.[38]

Finally, Kartomi views the concept of acculturation as a methodological problem. She explains that the etymology of the word can be defined as meaning "together." Acculturation also ignores how both cultures (of the oppressor and the oppressed) partake in the transformative process of transferring cultural identities. For example, Kartomi mentions that indicating that a child shares similar facial feature as his or her parents (eg., having "their mother's eyes") does not reveal anything meaningful about the identity of the child.[39]

If acculturation consists of myths and errors in relation to understanding cultures, then how does the theory of transculturation by Fernando Ortiz differ from other culture theories from the past? Ortiz concentrates primarily on the socioeconomic conditions in Cuba in the early decades in the twentieth century (up to 1940) and the diverse racial heritage on the island. He offers a condensed history of the distinct cultures in Cuba. Of the indigenous and European cultures in Cuba, he mentions that the native Indian (indigenous) transculturation resulted from the having to adapt to the Spanish European customs while also losing a part of the indigenous identity. In a similar manner, the Spanish who conquered the New World also underwent a transcultural process because they had to adjust to different geographical terrain and sociocultural environments.[40]

---

[38] Margaret J. Kartomi, 1981. In discussing European perceptions of non-Western cultures, one cannot assume that Europe did not care about cultures foreign to their own. Despite their many ethnocentric errors in judgement, printed books and documents concerning non-Western cultures aimed to educate European audiences about these foreign cultures in a way that *Europeans* comprehended them.

[39] Margaret J. Kartomi, 1981.

[40] Fernando Ortiz, "II. The Ethnography and Transculturation of Havanna Tobacco and the Beginnings of Sugar in America. 2: The Social Phenomenon of Transculturation and its Importance," en *Cuban Counterpoint, el Tobacco and Sugar* (Durham, NC: Duke University Press, 1940, 1995). 98.

Ortiz does not limit his condensed history of Cuba to only two cultures of the native Indians and Spanish colonists. He also mentions groups from Africa, other races and religious denominations who contributed to the development of the island. By doing this, Ortiz demonstrates that transculturation affects a plethora of cultures. Ortiz suggests that the African cultures became isolated from their original groups and their culture altered and destroyed (in Cuba). Ortiz also mentions the significant impact of immigration on the island. Several groups of immigrants that Ortiz mentions include the Indians of the continent, Jews, Portuguese, as well as groups from regions of China (what he refers to as the "Celestial Kingdom."). Ortiz indicates that these cultures in question, upon arriving in Cuba, encountered the same situation of mixing old and new cultures to create distinct identities in order to survive on the island.[41]

Ortiz illustrates in his work that transculturation involves more than merely acquiring the identity of an "advanced" culture and learning their social customs. Transculturation requires the combination of processes involving the loss of a submissive culture (indigenous and African) and gaining customs from a dominant culture (Europe and the United States). Through this combination, a new culture can coexist. However, Ortiz suggests that transculturated groups of people undergo some suffering and struggle by adjusting to their new identities.

The theory of transculturation by Fernando Ortiz has served many beneficial purposes for contemporary scholarship concerning Latin American studies. Ortiz has been praised for his development of this theory by anthropologists like Bronislow Malinowski (1884-1942). At the time of its introduction in the 1940s, Malinowski perceived transculturation as a positive theory that could help to establish positive diplomatic relations between Cuba and the United States.[42]

Other contemporary studies from the 1980s and 90s explore the concept of transculturation in *Cuban Counterpoint* from different perspectives. Antonio Benítez-Rojo (1931-2005) discusses the theory in relation to literature in his book *La isla que se repite: para una reinterpretación de la cultura caribeña (The Repeating Island: The Caribbean and the Postmodern*

---

[41] Fernando Ortiz, 98.
[42] Bronislow Malinowski, "Introduction," in *Cuban Counterpoint, Tabaco and Sugar* (New York: Alfred A. Knopf, 1947), xvi.

Perspective) (c. 1989): dedicating an entire chapter to the structure, content and impact of *Cuban Counterpoint*. Considering the time period in which Ortiz wrote that book (1940), Benítez-Rojo uses *Cuban Counterpoint* as a model for understanding its potential for revealing postmodern identities and analyses concerning Caribbean culture. He recommends that readers familiar with the book study it beyond the thematic material of the socioeconomic structures in Cuba. Benítez-Rojo suggests that these readers ought to also understand the postmodern view of the author as one who attempts to understand and improve his or her writing skills.[43]

José María Arguedas applies transculturation by referring to the impact of the indigenous communities in his native home of Peru in his book, *La formación de una cultura indoamericana (The Formation of an Indoamerican Culture)*(1969, 1975). Like Ortiz, Arguedas draws attention to the significance of the mixture of different races and cultures. Taking into consideration that Arguedas writes about these cultures from the perspective of an outsider, he still attempts to maintain a sense of respect for the indigenous Peruvian people.[44]

Ángel Rama applies the same theory of transculturation, albeit from the perspective of Latin American fictional literature. In his investigation from 1982, Rama concentrates primarily on the contemporary literary trends in Latin America at the beginning of the twentieth century, like Modernism versus Realism. Rama explains that the Avant-garde Latin American literature from the 1930s draws inspiration from European influences. Regionalist works from the 1910s, contrast, would derive inspiration from the local areas and different regions of Latin America.[45] Influenced by José María Arguedas, Rama discusses three components of what he calls "Transcultural Narratives.": Language,

---

[43] Antonio Benítez-Rojo y James E. Maraniss (English Transl.), "4. Fernando Ortiz: The Caribbean and Postmodernism," en *The Repeating Island: The Caribbean and the Postmodern Perspective, Second Edition* (Durham, NC: Duke University Press, 1996), 150-176.

[44] José María Arguedas, "El complejo cultural en el Perú," in *Formación de una cultura nacional Indoamericana*, (Coyoacán, MX: Siglo veintiuno editores, 1975), 1-9.

[45] José María Arguedas and Ángel Rama (Ed.), "Introducción," in *Formación de una cultura nacional Indoamericana*, (Coyoacán, MX: Siglo veintiuno editores, 1975), ix-xxiv; Ángel Rama and David Frye (English Transl.), "1. Literature and Culture," in *Writing Across Cultures: Narrative Transculturation in Latin America* (Durham, NC: Duke University Press, 2012), 3-36.

Literary Structure and Worldview. Focusing on these aspects of transcultural literature, he explains how authors would approach this writing style by combining specific regional Latin American dialects with contemporary language.[46]

---

[46] Ángel Rama and David Frye, 3-36.

"El ofrecer no empobrece."

("Offering does not impoverish.")

The Development of Transculturation: 1980s-2010s

Theorists who developed the theory of transculturation in the early decades of the twentieth century have concentrated predominantly on Latin American regions: specifically, the Hispanophone Caribbean. Considering that many scholars and investigators from the 1980s onward continue to apply this theory to this part of the world, one must also remember and comprehend the global nature of the theory of transculturation. Some publications, like research from Dharma Deva, Elfhria Arpoglou and others observe and apply this theory from outside the context of Latin America.[47] They frequently combine diverse theories with transculturation with the purpose of presenting clearer perspectives of the societies under scrutiny. As is the case with Dharma Deva, her study from 2000 examines transculturation in connection with the theory of acculturation. Given all of the aforementioned problems with that theory, it is possible that scholars like Margaret J. Kartomi would find the methodology behind such an investigation suspect.[48] Based on the studies compiled for this research, it deserves mention that applications of transculturation in the twentieth and twenty-first centuries include discussions related to politics, sociology and literature: with scant studies concentrating on music.

Diana Taylor discusses transculturation in terms of Latin American theater and drama.[49] In her 1991 article, "Transculturating Transculturation," Taylor explores more details about applying the theory within the context of sociological aspects. She mentions that the creation

---

[47] Eleftheria Arapoglou et al, *Mobile Narratives: Travel, Migration, and Transculturatio*(Nueva York: Routledge, 2013); Dharma Deva, "Musical Transculturation and Acculturation" http://www.rawa.asia/ethno/MUSICAL%20TRANSCULTURATION%20AND%20ACCULTURATION%20ESSAY.htm. 2000 (accessed October 25, 2015).

[48] Margaret J. Kartomi, "The Processes and Results of Musical Culture Contact: A Discussion of Terminology and Concepts," *Ethnomusicology* 25, No. 2 (1981), http://www.jstor.org/stable/851273 (accessed July 20, 2016).

[49] Diana Taylor, "Tranculturating Transculturation," *Performing Arts Journal* 13, No. 2 (May 1991), http://www.jstor.org/stable/3245476 (accessed September 21, 2015); *The Archive and the Repertoire: Performing Cultural Memory in the Americas*, (Durham, NC: Duke University Press, 2003).

and expansion of the theory by Fernando Ortiz and Ángel Rama (but, surprisingly, *not* José Maria Arguedas) serve as a blueprint for implementing transculturation from the point of view of theater.[50] By connecting the Latin American theatrical arts with this theory, Taylor preoccupies herself with helping her readers understand its repercussions. She illustrates this point in her investigation by indicating that transculturation can affect all parts of a culture; the processes behind the theory involve sociopolitical changes in addition to transformations in identity (individual, collective, verbal, and symbolic).[51]

In order for her readers to understand what the term "culture" signifies, Taylor devotes some time to defining the term. Citing David Laitin, Max Weber and Clifford Geerz, she explains that the term conveys sociopolitical meanings. She notes that culture enables people to establish and comprehend their identity.[52] She additionally expands the theory of transculturation beyond the original contexts established by Fernando Ortiz. While the theory indicates the creation of new cultures and identities through loss, gain and fusion, Taylor perceives transculturation as more than simply a process that promotes cultural miscegenation and unity (as Ortiz suggests in his work). Taylor indicates in her research that transculturation also carries political purposes through acquiring and applying power dynamics and tactics. Transculturation requires more than applying symbolism to understand identity. One must also consider and understand the political motivations for gaining power (eg., why the Spanish conquered the New World) and combining these identities: specifically, which cultural identities and philosophies serve to subjugate others.[53]

Taylor expresses in her research that it proves valuable to examine the theory of transculturation from different perspectives. She mentions that the process involved in this theory serves two main purposes. First, transculturation affects both cultures of the oppressor and the oppressed. Secondly, even though both cultures undergo the same transformation, the

---

[50] Diana Taylor, "Tranculturating Transculturation," *Performing Arts Journal* 13, No. 2 (May 1991), http://www.jstor.org/stable/3245476 (accessed September 21, 2015).
[51] Diana Taylor, 1991.
[52] Diana Taylor, 1991.
[53] Diana Taylor, 1991.

oppressing culture often refuses to candidly admit that their culture also changes. Taylor uses the terms "First World" and "Third World" in relation to Europe and the United States, who often tend to perceive certain regions of Latin America and the Caribbean in ethnocentric terms. The power struggle of "First World" versus "Third World" can also apply to Puerto with notable sociological programs, like "Operation Bootstrap" (*Operación manos a la obra*). The United States Government created this program in 1942 with the objectives of promoting social and economic reconstruction on the island of Puerto Rico, partially because the United States (which still functioned as an imperialist power at that time) saw the island as financially dependent on them for assistance.[54]

Other scholars, like Friedrich W. Sixel and José Luis González and Fabien Viala, also encounter errors and inconsistencies with the theory of transculturation in their investigation. Sixel focuses his study specifically on the case of the Landino indigenous community in Guatemala (1969) Towards the end of his ethnographic study, he concludes that the Landinos experienced trouble living and communicating with other indigenous groups in the country because the Landinos lost part of their original culture and modernized themselves in order to survive.[55] In relation to other problems with transculturation, according to Fabiene Viala in *The Post-Columbus Syndrome: National Culture and Commemoration in the Caribbean* (2014), she indicates that the theory tends to promote selective memory. To put another way, it functions by promoting memories that stress the European Spanish history and culture as the predominant factors in comprehending Latin American and Caribbean identities.[56]

---

[54] Déborah Berman Santana, ", *Revista Geográfica, 124* (1998). Puerto Rico's Operation Bootsrap: Colonial Roots of a Persistent Model for 'Third World' Development," *Revista Geografica* 124 (1998), http://www.jstor.org/stable/40992748 , (accessed October 30, 2016).

[55] Friedrich W. Sixel, "Cultural Inconsistencies in Transculturation Processes," *Sociologus 19*, No. 2 (1969), http://www.jstor.org/stable/43644408 (accessed June 6, 2016).

[56] Fabienne Viala. *El síndrome después de Colon: El nacionalismo cultural y conmemoraciones en el Caribe* (New York: Palgrave Macmillan, 2014), Libro en inglés.

José Luis González (1926-1996) also refuses to accept the theory of transculturation; his reasoning for this negation stems from the political conditions in Puerto Rico in the twentieth century (up to the late-1970s).

González perceives Puerto Rican history and culture from the perspective of an author rather than a historian. By applying Marxist principles, he completely denounces the United States occupation of Puerto Rico as a result of transcultural impact on the island: what he defines as "depuertoricanization." He interprets these causes and consequences more as a fight between "two cultures" in Puerto Rico.[57]

By contrast, Ernest A, Duff concentrates on the effects of United States Imperialism on the Puerto Rican economy in the 1980s. One intriguing aspect of this study is that Duff also devotes attention to modernization and transculturation in the rural mountainous areas of the island. Towards the end of his 1989 investigation, Duff presents several significant points. First, the inhabitants of the rural areas would often resist modernizing themselves in favor of maintaining their traditions and social customs. Second, Duff established that (as of the 1980s) remnants of transculturation propagated by United States Imperialism remain present in Puerto Rico.[58]

---

[57] José Luis González, "El país de cuatro pisos" in *El país de cuatro pisos y otros ensayos*, (Rio Piedras, PR: Ediciones Huracán, 1987), 34.
[58] Ernest A. Duff, "Transculturation in Puerto RicoLa transculturación en Puerto Rico: The Reality of An American Cultural Imperialism," *Caribbean Affairs* 2, No. 1 (1989), 116-128.

Table 1: Chronology and Comparison of Historical and Musical Events in Puerto Rico and Argentina: 1815-1945

Year/Decade	Event(s) in Puerto Rico	Event(s) in Argentina
1815	Royal Decree of Grace—law created by the Spanish Monarchy to advance the economy in Puerto Rico Permits foreigners from other Latin American and European countries to emigrate, reside and establish businesses in Puerto Rico.	Argentine independence from Spain (The Argentine War for Independence begins in 1810 and ends in 1818.)
1849	Publication of *The Gíbaro*, written by Manuel Alonso (1822-1889)	
1853		Abolition of slavery in Argentina and creation of the third Argentine Constitution
1868	Cry of Lares—a revolt against Spanish Imperialism	
1872-1880		Publications of the gaucho poems *The Gaucho Martín Fierro* (1872) and *The Return of Martín Fierro* (1879), written by José Hernández Publication of the gaucho novela novela *Juan Moreira* (1879-1880), written by Eduardo Gutiérrez
1873	Abolition of slavery in Puerto Rico	
1880-1914		Period of major economic growth and immigration to the country 1884: Competition between payadores

		Gabino Ezeiza and Juan de Nava
1889	Publication of the book, *The Puerto Rican Cuntryman: His Physical Conditions, Intellect and Morals, Determining Causes, and Means for Improvement*, written by Francisco del Valle Atiles	
1894		The first documented competition between payadores Gabino Ezeiza and Pablo Vázquez
1895-1898	Spanish-American War United States occupation of Puerto Rico	
1899	Hurricane San Ciriaco—causes widespread damage to island and leads to mass migration to parts of the United States: most notably, Hawaii	
1900	Foraker Act—established a (limited) Democratic Puerto Rican government	March 30: By presidential decree, words in the Argentine national anthem that are considered offensive to Spanish immigrants are omitted in public presentations.
1890s-1910s	The first musical recordings on wax cylinders, and later, on phonographic discs 1909-1910: Period of recordings of Puerto Rican folk music created in Puerto Rico and the United States	The first musical recordings on wax cylinders, and later, on phonographic disks 1900s: Factories and studios for creating and recording music in Argentina established
1914-1918	World War I 1917: Jones-Shafroth Act—enforces Unites States citizenship on	World War I 1914: Population of Argentina is at 7,900,000 people.

		Puerto Ricans, who also get drafted into military service in the war.	58% of this population consists of European immigrants.[59]
		Victor Records visits Puerto Rico	1916: Publication of book, *The payador*, written by Leopoldo Lugones (in relation to Argentine gaucho literature)
			1917: Premiere of the first (known) tango canción, "Mi noche' triste" ("My Sad Night")
	1920	"Radio Porto Rico Club" established	August 27: The first radio broadcast in Argentina
	1922	December 3: Inauguration of the first radio station (WKAQ) in San Juan, PR	
	1928	Hurricane San Felipe	
	1929	Great Depression Beginning of radio shows	Great Depression Beginning of radio shows *The Face of the Wolf*, one of the first Argentine radio novelas
	1930	*The Andalusian Horse*, a radio novela with daily episodes	September 6: "The Infamous Decade" Censorship of radio with strict rules
	1932	Hurricane San Ciprian	(1932-1935) Chaco War
	1933-1946	Unemployment at 65%-- "The Dead Times" New Deal PRERA founded	1933: First Rules of Radio Communications Censorship of slang language in music

---

[59] El observador: "Mi noche triste." "Cien años atrás, Gardel estrenaba el primer tango canción de la historia," *Perfil*, http://www.perfil.com/elobservador/cien-anos-atras-gardel-estrenaba-el-primer-tango-cancion-de-la-historia.phtml, el 7 de enero de 2017 (accessed April 13, 2018).

1934	Chardón Plan Sugar cane strike Second radio station (WNEL) established in San Juan	
1935-1936	Administrative Reconstruction (PRRA) Docks Strike April 1935: Carlos Gardel tours Puerto Rico	Golden age of tango—ends in 1955 Publication of the tango canción "Cambalache," by Enrique Santos Discépolo May 1936: Inauguration of the Obelisque, to celebrate the four-hundredth anniversary of the founding of Argentina
1939-45	World War II	World War II
1942-43	Creation of the governmental program "Operation Bootstrap"	1943: Coup d'etat in Argentina, the country governed under the dictatorship of Juan Perón Tango canción "Cambalache" suffers censorship by the Ministry of Education
1945	World War II ends.	World War II ends. Publication of book, *The Infamous Decade* by the journalist, author and politician José Luis Torres.

Table 2: Investigations on the Theory of Transculturation

People and Profession	Country	Year(s) of Contribution	Description
Fernando Ortiz: anthropologist, criminologist and Spiritist	Cuba	1940	Creates theory of *transculturation*, or the process of creating a new culture by combining two preexisting ones Involves series of cultural loss of one culture and gain of another Perceives his theory as a better alternative to *acculturation* (1930s), or the imposed transformation from one culture to another
Bronislow Molinowski: anthropologist	United States	1940	Promotes theory of transculturation by Ortiz
José María Arguedas: author	Perú	1969, 1975 (Post.)	Applies transculturation to Latin American literature by concentrating on the native Peruvian culture
Ángel Rama: author	Uruguay	1982	Expands upon the literary aspects of transculturation
Friedrich W. Sixel: antropologist	Germany	1969	Discusses the sociological effects of transculturation in Guatemala through a case study of the Landino (Indian-Guatemalan) community

José Luis González: author	Puerto Rico	1979	Refutes transculturation in Puerto Rico in relation to the United States' occupation of the Caribbean island from 1898 to 1952
Margaret J. Kartomi: ethnomusicologist	Australia	1981	Applies transculturation within the musical context of performance practice Perceives the term as a better alternative to *acculturation*: a term which she views as ambiguous and hackneyed in cultural studies Cites Fernando Ortiz, but does not consider the gaps and presence of racial biases in his theory
Ernest A. Duff, anthropologist	United States	1989	Discusses transculturation within the context of the Puerto Rican economy at the time of the North American occupation of the island and in the 1980s
Diana Taylor: anthropologist, historian, specialist in Latin American Theater	Mexico, United States	1991	Applies transculturation to Latin American theater

| Fabienne Viala, anthropologist, specialist in Latin American history and cultural studies | Great Britain | 2014 | Dismisses transculturation because of its application as a component of selective cultural memory |

"Pueblo pequeño, campana grande"
("Small town, big bell")

Technology of the Times

<u>Radio in Puerto Rico and Argentina</u>

"Radio has brought the best music of the world closer to all people who want to hear it and have access to a receiver."
-From a radio reporter and fan-

("La radio ha acercado la mejor música del mundo a todas las personas que deseen escucharla y tengan acceso a un aparato receptor.")
-de un locutor aficionado-

In the 1920s, the creation of radio transmission technology emerged. The inaugural radio broadcast in Argentina began on August 27, 1920. The transmission at the Coliseum Theater of Buenos Aires (Teatro Coliseo de Buenos Aires), which lasted for three hours, began with these words: "Ladies and gentlemen: Today, the Argentine Radio Society presents the sacred festival of Richard Wagner's *Parsifal...*" ("Señoras y señores: La Sociedad Radio Argentina les presenta hoy el festival sacro de Ricardo Wagner *Parsifal...*"). This broadcast was made possible through the dedication and work from four university medical students and radio fanatics known as "Los locos de Azotea." ("The Crazy People on the Rooftop").[60]

---

[60] Mdz, "Historia cronológica de la radio en Argentina."
https://www.mdzol.com/nota/232937-historia-cronologica-de-la-radio-en-la-

| Fabienne Viala, anthropologist, specialist in Latin American history and cultural studies | Great Britain | 2014 | Dismisses transculturation because of its application as a component of selective cultural memory |

"Pueblo pequeño, campana grande"
("Small town, big bell")

Technology of the Times

<u>Radio in Puerto Rico and Argentina</u>

"Radio has brought the best music of the world closer to all people who want to hear it and have access to a receiver."
-From a radio reporter and fan-

("La radio ha acercado la mejor música del mundo a todas las personas que deseen escucharla y tengan acceso a un aparato receptor.")
-de un locutor aficionado-

In the 1920s, the creation of radio transmission technology emerged. The inaugural radio broadcast in Argentina began on August 27, 1920. The transmission at the Coliseum Theater of Buenos Aires (Teatro Coliseo de Buenos Aires), which lasted for three hours, began with these words: "Ladies and gentlemen: Today, the Argentine Radio Society presents the sacred festival of Richard Wagner's *Parsifal*…" ("Señoras y señores: La Sociedad Radio Argentina les presenta hoy el festival sacro de Ricardo Wagner *Parsifal*…"). This broadcast was made possible through the dedication and work from four university medical students and radio fanatics known as "Los locos de Azotea." ("The Crazy People on the Rooftop").[60]

---

[60] Mdz, "Historia cronológica de la radio en Argentina." https://www.mdzol.com/nota/232937-historia-cronologica-de-la-radio-en-la-

In 1920, Puerto Rico also featured a group of radio aficionados called, "Porto Rico Radio Club": directed by Joaquín Agusty and Manolo Ochoa in addition to other club members. This new technology arrived on the island on December 3, 1922 with an inaugural program from WKAQ in San Juan. It included these first words on the radio waves: "This is WKAQ in San Juan, the capital of Puerto Rico, the Island of Enchantment, and where the best coffee in the world is produced!" ["Esta es WKAQ en San Juan, capital de Puerto Rico, La Isla del Encanto, y donde se produce el mejor café del mundo." (Joaquín Agusty)]. The short program began with the Puerto Rican national anthem "La Borinqueña," commemorative speeches by the judge of the Supreme Tribunal Emilio Toro Cuevas, brief words from the manager of the telephone company J. T. Quinn, followed by musical selections which included a soprano and pianist interpreting *danza* music.[61]

Relatively few radio receivers existed on the island in the early twentieth century. The process of global transmission was long and experimental. In the early years of radio, broadcasts were initially raw, unedited and transmitted live. Over time, radio gradually converted into a grand instrument for transcultural communication, which enabled the possibility for immigrants to integrate this new sociocultural aspect. It deserves mention that fifty people listened to the initial radio transmission in Argentina, the number of owned radios in the country at that time. Radio evolved rapidly that, by 1923, Argentina had sixty-thousand radio receivers. That same year, radio stations began creating names by combining letters and numbers under the direction of the Ministry of Marina.[62] Taking these factors into consideration, radio in Argentina arrived and expanded to public audiences in 1926. In Puerto Rico, radio

---

argentina/ (accessed March 12, 2018); Héctor Benedetti, "4. Problemático y febril: Un camino ascendente entre dos crisis de expresión," en *Nueva historia del tango: De los orígenes al siglo XXI* (Buenos Aires: Siglo XXI Editores, 2016), 124-128.

[61] Tinta digital, "La radioafición en Puerto Rico," http://www.qsl.net/kp4md/rcprsp.htm (accessed March 12, 2018); "Comienzos de la radio en Puerto Rico," http://tintadigitalpr.com/blog/comienzos-de-la-radio-en-puerto-rico/ (accessed March 12, 2018).

[62] Héctor Benedetti, "4. Problemático y febril: Un camino ascendente entre dos crisis de expresión," en *Nueva historia del tango: De los orígenes al siglo XXI* (Buenos Aires: Siglo XXI Editores, 2016), 124-128.

aficionados transmitted phonographic records to entertain their friends. By the 1930s on the island, the availability of radios grew to four thousand and an audience of twenty-five thousand people.[63]

In Argentina, radio continued to expand; several radio stations were created within mere days of each other, like Radio Argentina and Radio Cultura. The following is a list of many of the radio stations established: Radio Nacional LRA, Radio Paris, Radio Belgrano LR4 Radio "Splendid." The first Puerto Rican radio station, WKAQ in 1922, was followed in 1934 by WNEL as the second radio station in San Juan, which specialized in radio show productions. Later, other radio stations formed on different areas of the island: like, WPRP Ponce in 1936 and WPRA Mayagüez in 1937.[64]

Even though people did not originally perceive radio as a commercial institution, Argentina inaugurated the radio station LV10 Radio Cuyo in 1931. It was the first Argentine commercial radio station, specializing in sales and entertainment. This radio station transmitted prerecorded music and announcements, as well as invited musicians to perform in the studio. The station WNEL in Puerto Rico implemented radio theater. It was the first radio station to subscribe to an agency of news outside of Puerto Rico and to bring foreign musical artists to present themselves on programs as invited international guests (eg., Jorge Negrete and Pedro Vargas from Mexico).[65]

Receivers

The new radio technology allowed for neighbors to create a sense of camaraderie when they gathered to hear their favorite programs for entertainment: music, comedy, drama, and sporting event broadcasts. Owning a radio receiver in Puerto Rico and Argentina in the 1920s and

---

[63] Mdz, "Historia cronológica de la radio en Argentina." https://www.mdzol.com/nota/232937-historia-cronologica-de-la-radio-en-la-argentina/ (accessed March 12, 2018); "Comienzos de la radio en Puerto Rico," http://tintadigitalpr.com/blog/comienzos-de-la-radio-en-puerto-rico/ (accessed March 12, 2018).

[64] "Historia cronológica de la radio en Argentina"; "Comienzos de la radio en Puerto Rico,"

[65] "Historia cronológica de la radio en Argentina"; "Comienzos de la radio en Puerto Rico,"

30s often proved difficult because of socioeconomic and political strife. The crash of the Stock Market and global economy in 1929, natural disasters and political turmoil complicated matters concerning social living in both regions.[66] For example, in those times, the weekly compensation for a worker in Puerto Rico amounted to ten to twelve dollars. When the cost of radio receivers fluctuated between thirty and seventy dollars, people often considered this device a luxury item.

One consequence of the new radio technology in Puerto Rico stemmed from the necessity for receiver repairmen: a common problem with radios sold on the island. Courses were developed for the purpose of teaching aspiring radio technicians. When students enrolled in these courses, they received diagrams, plans and guides as part of their instruction.[67] As a result, these tools and instructions enabled people to construct their own radios: many of them noticeably secondhand quality and defective. People could purchase radio receivers at furniture stores, like La Casa Sánchez Morales, which dedicated part of its business to selling receivers for more than twenty years. From 1945 to 1950, one could find different brands of receivers like *Zenith*, *Philco* and *RCA*.[68]

What Radio Listeners Waited For

Radio receivers, which were initially heavy and designed for placing on tables, often came in furniture styles or simple designs. If one raised the volume, the neighbors who did not have radios could also benefit from the entertainment. On the radio transmissions, one encountered genres and formats well received by listeners. In Argentina, listeners frequently heard daily broadcasts of classical music. The daily news also earned programming space through live transmission. 1923 gave way to the "Boxing Fight of the Century," and in 1924 the Soccer (Futbol) match between Uruguay and Argentina.[69]

---

[66] "Comienzos de la radio en Puerto Rico"
[67] "Comienzos de la radio en Puerto Rico"
[68] "Comienzos de la radio en Puerto Rico"
[69] Mundo Sur 106.5, "Historia de la radio en Argentina,"
http://www.mundosurfm.com/historia-de-la-radio-en-la-argentina/ (accessed March 12, 2018).

Radio Theater (radio shows) maintained popularity like in Puerto Rico. The first programs served as combinations of creole music concentrating on folk songs, payadas and comedies. Scholars attribute Francisco Mastandrea to changing the format to focus on dramas in what called the *novela* with his creation *La caricia del lobo* (*The Face of the Wolf*): a radio novela which continued in sequence daily with a thematic structure and gaucho drama. In 1930 on the island of Puerto Rico, the first radio novela premiered entitled, *El caballo andaluz* (*The Andalusian Horse*). Many radio listeners considered this production to have a rustic and primitive format for those days (of "bad quality").[70]

Comedy and satire proved popular forms of entertainment in Puerto Rico. In 1932, the program *Compay Sico y Compay Telo*, which later changed to the political satire *Los jíbaros de la radio* (*The Jíbaros of the Radio*), rose to prominence. The members of this program from 1930 to 1939 were Manolin Martínez, "Manomeco" (the fictional character created by Jesús Rivera Pérez) and Modesto Navarro. The opening and closing themes for the show were performed by the folk music group "Aurora."[71]

Additionally, radio stations (in Puerto Rico) introduced and played a plethora of folk music, like the program *La hora campesina* (*The Countrymen's Hour*) from 1937. New musical talents emerged like Juan Antonio "Toñin" Romero Muñiz from the town of Jayuya; who, at the age of ten, formed part of the artistic roster on the radio station WPRP. For the 1940s, *Melodías criollas* (*Creole Melodies*) emerged on WKAQ with the participation of the Maorales Ramos brothers from Caguas: Ramito, Moralito y Luisito who at twelve years old performed his first décima on the radio.

The Governments and Radio Programming

The consequences of economic crises and governmental reform created a sense of restlessness in the cities and towns, affecting the media and forms of deriving information and communication, like the Press and radio. As part of this form of governance in Argentina, those in power

---

[70] Tinta Digital PR, "Comienzos de la radio en Puerto Rico," http://tintadigitalpr.com/blog/comienzos-de-la-radio-en-puerto-rico/ (accessed March 12, 2018).

[71] Tinta Digital PR, "Comienzos de la radio en Puerto Rico."

enforced censorship and strict rules. In 1933, the Argentine Government established Regulations for Radio Communication, which went into effect until May 1946. In that year, Edelmiro Farrell presented another decree and manual of instructions for radio broadcasting: a compilation of the rules written in 1933. Reasoning and motivations behind governmental censorship of music on the radio ranged from politics, language, paranoia, and ridiculousness.[72]

From 1930 to 1943, the period which many Argentine historians refer to as "The Infamous Decade" ("La Década Infame"), Argentina suffered a series of instability and outrage in the workforce. In his retrospective book from 1945 *The Infamous Decade* (*La Década Infame*), the journalist, author and politician José Luis Torres expressed his views on the electoral fraud and corruption of the times.[73] Several of the stringent rules for implementing censorship in radio came in the form of banning certain words. According to Enrique Fraga in his book, *La prohibición del lunfardo en la radiodifusión* (*The Prohibition of Slang in Radio Broadcasts*); this included words like "broadcast," "national," "thug," and "milonga." According to the author, the definition of "milonga" (in terms of political censorship) meant directly crossing out emblems and popular worldviews. This restrictive situation arrived at a point where some radio stations either had to shut down or change their name so that they could continue transmitting content.[74] One descriptive model divulging the matters at that point in time is the tango canción "Cambalache." Looking at this song from the perspective of the past, one notices that during "The Infamous Decade," this tango survived for eight years without undergoing censorship.

In the period from 1943 to 1949, the decree of the manual of instructions for radio transmission became systematically put into practice. The Ministry of Education in that era, after carefully analyzing the lyrics to

---

[72] Juan Pablo Bertazza, "Si se calla el cantor," *Página 12*,
https://www.pagina12.com.ar/diario/suplementos/radar/9-4990-2008-12-14.html (accessed April 18, 2018).
[73] Gregorio Selser, "Prohíbese el tango 'Cambalache,' escrito en 1935. Molesto espejo." *El Dia*, 26 de octubre de 1981, 55.
[74] Mdz, "Historia cronológica de la radio en Argentina."
https://www.mdzol.com/nota/232937-historia-cronologica-de-la-radio-en-la-argentina/ (accessed March 12, 20182018): Enrique Fraga, *La prohibición del lunfardo en la radiodifusión* (Argentina: Lajouane, 2006).

"Cambalache," censored the tango for promoting acts of Sedition and what they understood as bad interpretation of the Argentine language through slang. In 1976, "Cambalache" underwent new censorship: that time, under the military dictatorship of the era. Approximately eighty-three years have passed since the composition of this tango canción, and it is still adapted to the present times and offers a predominantly pessimistic reflection on the future. It is for this reason that Gegorio Selser uses "Cambalache" in 1981 to analyze and criticize another period of crisis in Argentina.[75]

Meanwhile, on the island of Puerto Rico, the government developed a complementary project designed to educate listeners called, "La Escuela del Aire." ("School on the Airwaves"). This program began in 1935, consisting of a time slot dedicated to all main radio stations on the island. Stations from San Juan, Ponce and Mayagüez retransmitted educational programs, in addition to a night program devoted to entertaining the general public and educating adults. These programs promoted methods for combating illiteracy, helped contribute to socialization in the rural areas, provided information related to economic affairs, civic social problems, and agriculture among others. This project formed a model for educational radio programming for encouraging teaching and activities for the population of youths and adults.[76] Among the people who assisted in this programming, one encountered authors like Enrique Laguerre and Julia de Burgos and actors like Lucy Boscana and Leopoldo Santiago Lavadero. This served as the base for what would later lead to the governmental public radio station WIPR. Ernesto Ramos Antonini initiated this program.[77]

---

[75] Gregorio Selser, "Prohíbese el tango 'Cambalache,' escrito en 1935. Molesto espejo." *El Día*, 26 de octubre de 1981, 55.
[76] Tinta Digital PR, "Comienzos de la radio en Puerto Rico," http://tintadigitalpr.com/blog/comienzos-de-la-radio-en-puerto-rico/ (accessed March 12, 2018).
[77] Tinta Digital PR, "Comienzos de la radio en Puerto Rico."

Musical Recordings

The creation and expansion of music became possible partially because of the global diffusion through new ideas and technological rebirth. This occurred when apparatuses designed for transmitting sound appeared in the everyday life, applying more advanced forms of technology as time changed. In 1877, Thomas Edison created the phonograph, which used wax cylinders to record dictation and (later) music. With the implementation of cylinders in Argentina in the 1890s, the production establishments offered distinct selections of lyrical pieces, patriotic songs and music by payadores.[78]

Emil Berliner created the gramophone in 1888. This invention imposed itself over the phonograph, using flat records (78 RPM) instead of wax cylinders. Already by 1894, recording technology companies had launched records into production. However, as it occurred in most parts of the world, cylinders and discs coexisted until most of these manufacturing plants became obsolete and disappeared. Additionally, people found it logical for new technology to replace older formats. The advantages that a record had over a wax cylinder stemmed from greater space for reproduction, based on how disc formats would keep evolving over time. Records could include more seconds or minutes, and later allowed for two sound recordings: one on each side.[79]

Record companies began to emerge, like Columbia Records, Victor Records, Odeon—later Disco Nacional among others. This brief journey into technology would not be complete without mentioning the performers who served to create and enliven the atmosphere of recordings. One of the first musicians who grew in popularity through this form of media was Vicente Greco. Greco worked for Columbia Records and had a catalog of tangos where, for the first time, he applied the term "repertorio criollo" ("Creole Repertoire"). By 1904, Carlos Gardel also appeared on the music catalog from Columbia Records.[80]

---

[78] Héctor Benedetti, "3. Setenta y ocho revoluciones por minuto: El tango empieza a expandirse," en *Nueva historia del tango: De los orígenes al siglo XXI* (Buenos Aires: Siglo XXI Editores, 2015), 87-113.
[79] Héctor Benedetti, 87-113.
[80] Héctor Benedetti, 87-113.

Carlos Gardel and José Razzano also signed onto other record labels like Disco Nacional. This is solely to mention some of the hundreds of outstanding musicians who used this new technology. Political situations and the development of World War I (1914-1918) transformed the destiny of nations, and these factors affected the discographies in Argentina. Records were recorded in Buenos Aires, but the manufacturing plants for pressing and reproducing these records were in Europe. Having great demand for a commodity and short supply, production remained disproportionate.[81]

Information concerning the first musical recordings in Puerto Rico in the 1900s and 1910s indicates several hiatuses in its chronology. It deserves mention that, at that point in time. Puerto Rico spent over ten years as an imperial territory under the United States. In recent years, a wax cylinder recording from the Edison Amberol company from 1909 was found. It features music performed by Gracia López: the first female to record music outside of Puerto Rico, a *guaracha*. Some recordings from this era survive, but these are encountered in private collections not open to the public.[82]

According to the music recording collector David Morales, few record companies travelled to Puerto Rico or recorded music from that island. In 1910, in the case of *Columbia Records*, that company travelled to San Juan, where they produced more than one hundred recordings. However, one can quickly count the small number of recordings of traditional folk music (música jíbara). The record company *Victor* also visited the island. The catalog from the Library of Congress in Washington, DC features only six recordings released by Victor in 1917, which primarily contains chamber music.[83]

The fourth volume from the book series entitled, *Ethnic Music on Records: A Discography of Ethnic Recordings Produced in the United States, 1893-1942*, written by Richard K. Spottswood, covers a period of nearly fifty years of audio recordings and preservation. Spottswood dedicates this

---

[81] Héctor Benedetti, 87-113.
[82] David Morales, "Early Audio-Recordings of Puerto Rican Jíbaro Music: 1909-1910." *La Clave* (Blog), http://plenama.blogspot.com/2011/06/early-audio-recordings-of-puerto-rican.html?m=1 (accessed March 14, 2018).
[83] Library of Congress, "Audio Recordings, 1910-1919, Puerto Rico," https://www.loc.gov/audio/?fa=location%3Apuerto+rico&dates=1910-1919 (accessed March 24, 2018).

specific volume to Spanish cultures, including areas from Latin America, the Caribbean (Puerto Rico), Portugal, Philippines, and Basque region of Spain.[84] In relation to Puerto Rico, the catalog from Spottswood consist of a diversity of included recordings: four danzas, coplas, tipiccas, jíbaro dances, three songs, and a guaracha. It is here where the "seis chorreao" gets described as a rapid melody performed by the cuatro as accompaniment to a décima. The seis here refers to the dance, not the song and type of music. Also, Spottswood provides in his catalog names of singers, groups and orchestras like Orquesta Cocolía, Orquesta Tizol and Orquesta Andino and Parrilla among others.[85] It deserves brief mention that the Ansona record label specialized in producing trova countryside music.

A Transcultural Link with Technology

Musical recordings, radio and radio theater contributed notably to the creation of a transcultural link, where the listening public enthusiastically had preferences for their favorite trovadors like Toñin Romero, the Morales Ramos Brothers and German Rosario among others. Folk music from Puerto Rico and Argentina expanded around the world, and the music from Argentina increased in popularity on the island of Puerto Rico. Some of the trovadores mention previously in this study, have been credited for creating some of the seis inspired by music from Argentina. Additionally, it deserves mention that Mariano Cotto from the town of Naranjito, who is known by many as "The Beat of the Espinela" (el "Bate de la espinela") for his application of the "forced foot" ("pie forzado") which is used to partially describe difficult rhyming techniques. Many credit Cotto for the "tanguillo" and "música campera" styles of the seis. Groups of Puerto Rican musicians had migrated to New York by the

---

[84] Richard K. Spottswood, *Ethnic Music on Records: A Discography of Ethnic Recordings Produced in the United States: 1893-1942—Volume 4: Spanish, Portuguese, Filipino, Basque* (Urbana, IL: University of Illinois Press, 1990), 1609-2412.

[85] Ricardo K. Spottswood, 1609-2412; "Early Audio-Recordings of Puerto Rican Jíbaro Music: 1909-1910." *La Clave* (Blog), http://plenama.blogspot.com/2011/06/early-audio-recordings-of-puerto-rican.html?m=1 (accessed March 14, 2018).
http://plenama.blogspot.com/2011/06/early-audio-recordings-of-puerto-rican.html?m=1 (acceso el 14 de marzo de 2018).

1930s. The Flores Cuartet (Cuarteto Flores, led by Pedro Flores) recorded the song "Aguinaldo trulla": a recording of stylized folk music. Later, this process came to be known as "The Birth of the Urban Jíbaro" ("El nacimiento del jíbaro urbano"). Other favorite musicians included Chuito from Cayey, Chuito from Bayamón and the group Aurora among other musical artists.[86]

The tango also entered a period of splendor, with lyricists, singers and musicians like Omero Manzi, Osvaldo Pugliese Anibal Troillo, y Carlos Gardel, who proved to be a favorite for many listeners. With the "Gardel Mania" spreading across radio stations, people established fan groups on the island of Puerto Rico. Radio station WNEL, as well as other forms of media, took charge of promoting news about Gardel and his visit to the island in April 1935. Unfortunately, the same media divulged the tragic news of his death that same year to Puerto Rican audiences. The appreciation for Carlos Gardel and Argentine tango created a sense of unity for people who loved this type of music. In the 1940s, radio and radio theater continued to serve as the format for receiving local and foreign musical artists. Tango music expanded in popularity in the Puerto Rican community through the years, with innumerable groups of fans who emulated the style of that period.

This last aspect manifested itself so much that the comedic radio show *Jíbaros de la radio* (*Jíbaros of the Radio*) produced an episode with special guest appearance from Argentine singer Libertad Lamarque. In order to establish an idea of the relationship between the two cultures (Puerto Rico and Argentina), Jesús Rivera Pérez wrote a folk comedy skit, where Libertad Lamarque participated and performed. According to the script, Libertad claimed that she was a Puerto Rican descendant, and "Manomeco" would call her a liar. She established that she was born on the island of Vieques, and she was looking for her brother so could cook *mofongo* (mashed plantains stuffed with meats and vegetables) and *cuchifritos* (a type of stew) for him. In the parody, she frequently mentioned that she was from the island of Vieques (a place where she had never been). This parody demonstrates a transcultural connection between the two countries with direct references to the daily customs on the island and an application of Puerto Rican dialectical speech.

---

[86] Proyecto del Cuatro Puertorriqueño, "Trovadores puertorriqueños," http://www.cuatro-pr.org/es/node/150 (accessed April 8, 2018).

Later, in 1946, Libertad Lamarque decided to visit the island of Vieques. To her surprise, she was declared the "Adopted Daughter" of Vieques by the then-Mayor Antonio Avila. She developed a great sense of admiration for Puerto Rico and the sister island of Vieques. In her long career, she visited the island of Puerto Rico countless times.

"El que siembra cosecha."
("He reaps what he sows.")

Origins and Structure of the Puerto Rican Seis

I dance the seis and the chain
when in the land of Macarena (Spain)
the most virtuosic dancer could dance a *zapateado*;
I have elements of poetry
to the tune of the voice of the *tiple*
beautiful décimas without number, as flowers bloom in the garden.

(Yo bailo el seis y la cadena
con en la tierra macarena
puede bailar un zapateado el más donoso bailarín;
tengo ribetes de coplero,
y al son del tiple vocinglero,
décimas bellas da ni numen, como da flores el jardín.)[87]

-Virgilio Davila

The book *Voz folklórica de Puerto Rico (Puerto Rican Folkloric Voice)* by poet and author Cesáreo Rosa-Nieves (1901-1974) serves as a brief study about the oral and popular traditions, where he also includes a discussion about the art of dance on the island. While he concentrates part of this study on the already archaic colonial decades (before 1898), like the *contradanza* ("country dance") and much later what people now understand as the Puerto Rican *danza*, Rosa Nieves dedicates part of his investigation to explaining the origins of the Puerto Rican seis.[88] Before beginning a discussion about the seis, however, it is imperative to direct attention to interpretations of the seis: the seis as a dance and the seis as music. To

---

[87] Virgilio Davila, "El jíbaro," Poem Hunter, https://www.poemhunter.com/poem/el-j-baro/comments/ (accessed March 3, 2018).

[88] Cesáreo Rosa-Nieves, "Los Bailes de Puerto Rico." *Revista del Instituto de Cultura Puertorriqueña* No. 65, 1974, 14-18, https://issuu.com/coleccionpuertorriquena/docs/primera_serie_n__mero_65 (accessed February 20, 2018).

clarify these differences and avoid confusion, this section will begin with a discussion concerning how people applied the seis in the past.

The Seis as a Dance

The Puerto Rican seis is often perceived as synonymous with the folkloric culture of the rural jíbaro, taking into consideration the plethora of categories and musical forms: like the "Seis Chorreao," or "Seis Fajardeño." In recent decades, musicologists and ethnomusicologists like Pedro and Elsa Escabi (1976)[89] and Jaime Bofil (2013)[90] have attempted to classify this type of music. Many other sources refer to the seis as a form of Puerto Rican music that flourished in the decades of the nineteenth century.

Sources closely related to the culture and music of Puerto Rico by Cesáreo Rosa Nieves cite the renowned Puerto Rican musicologist Francisco López Cruz (1907-1988). Studies by López Cruz indicate that the seis originated in Spain in the region of Andalusia in the 1600s and 1700s.[91] The application of the seis as a dance in those times served a religious function and not a secular form of entertainment. By the 1840s, the significance of the dance in the religious seis began to transform into a secular format.

To illustrate this last point, I refer to two excerpts from the nineteenth-century written works by Manuel Alonso and Francisco Valle Atiles. Even though his description is not entirely accurate, Manuel Alonso does provide a few correct details related to the seis as a dance in the Puerto Rican jíbaro community. The following is his description for how to dance the seis:

> The seis, although strictly speaking should be danced with six pairs, I have seen many more;

---

[89] Pedro C Escabi y Elsa M. Escabi, *La décima: Vista parcial del folklore*. Rio Piedras, PR: Editorial Universitaria. Universidad de Puerto Rico, 1976.

[90] Jaime O. Bofil-Calero, "Chapter 3: The Seis," in *Improvisation in Jíbaro Music: A Structural Analysis*, Tuscon, AZ: University of Arizona, 2013, PhD Dissertation.

[91] Cesáreo Rosa-Nieves, "Los Bailes de Puerto Rico." *Revista del Instituto de Cultura Puertorriqueña* No. 65, 1974, 14-18, https://issuu.com/coleccionpuertorriquena/docs/primera_serie_n_mero_65 (accessed February 20, 2018).

women are placed in front of men in rows,
they cross several times, stomp on one pass
on certain measures marked by the music
and end by waltzing, the same as in the contradance.
After this chain, the seis is one of the most beloved
dances of the *garabato*, because it is not thunderous
like the *son*: solid, but not cold like the fandanguillo
and the *caballo*...

(El seis, aunque en rigor deben bailarle
seis parejas, yo he visto muchas más; colócanse
las mujeres frente a los hombres en
hileras, se cruzan varias veces, zapatean un
paso en ciertos compases marcados por la
música y terminan valsando, lo mismo que en
la contradanza. Después de las cadenas, el
seis es de los bailes de garabato el que más
gusta, porque no es atronador como el son·
duro, ni frío como el fandanguillo y el caballo ...)[92]

With this description, one can clearly grasp how the jíbaro from the rural areas of Puerto Rico in the 1840s interpreted the dance. According to Alonso, the strict form of the seis as a dance involves six pairs of men and women. The reason why some sources refer to the seis as a precursor to the contradanza stems from how both share similar dance steps. His explanation of the directions is specific in how the men and women approach the dance: crossing, stomping, etc.[93]

Forty years after Manuel Alnsonso (1889) Francisco del Valle Atiles mentions the seis as a dance in pessimistic terms in his ethnographic study. In this work, Valle Atiles concentrates more on the religious purpose behind the dance segment of the seis. He laments the original

---

[92] Cesáreo Rosa-Nieves, 14-18; Manuel Alonso, "Escena V. Bailes de Puerto-Rico," in *El gíbaro: Cuadro de costumbres de la isla de Puerto-Rico* (Barcelona: D. Juan Oliveres, 1849) 55-68 (accessed el 14 abril de 2015), Public domain.

[93] Manuel Alonso, 55-68.

context of the seis, which (by his time) completely changed and became secular. According to the author:

> ...The *seis*, so named in remembrance of the seis where people danced before an altar, according to a Christian ritual already forgotten, it is a dance of figures, of true grace, which is gradually losing recollection of the antique dance, of figures like the Spanish, substituted today for the sensual *merengue*, which also adjusts itself to the *seis*...

> (...El *seis*, así llamado acaso en recuerdo de los seises que bailaban delante de los altares, según un rito cristiano ya olvidado, es un baile de figuras, de cierto donaire, que es sensible vaya perdiendo sus reminiscencias de la antigua danza, de figuras como la española, hoy sustituida por el *merengue* sensual, al que también se ajusta el *seis*...)[94]

Based on this quote, the description by Valle Atiles stands out when he indicates that the seis began as a form where "... people danced before an altar..."[95] What possible sources corroborate this information? Investigations into this question reveal that the sacred dance form of the seis refers to a religious practice used in Spain as part of the celebration of the Festival of Corpus Christi in the Spanish Conquest and colonial period. The Spanish Andalusians brought the seis (as a dance form) to the New World.[96] Puerto Rican historian Salvador Brau (1842-1912) confirms this information in his respective work entitled, *Historia de Puerto Rico* (*History of Puerto Rico*):

> In the Corpus (Christi) one observed in Puerto Rico the original custom from Sevilla, where it was practiced there by choirs of children

---

[94] Francisco del Valle Atiles, *El campesino puertorriqueño: sus condiciones físicas, intelectuales y morales, causas que las determinan y medios para mejorarlas.* (San Juan: Tipo de Gonzales Font, 1889), 71, https://freeditorial.com/es/books/el-campesino-puertorriqueno-sus-condiciones-fisicas-intelectuales-y-morales/related-books (accessed February 4, 2018), Public Domain.

[95] Francisco del Valle Atiles, 1889.

[96] Cesáreo Rosa-Nieves, "Los Bailes de Puerto Rico." *Revista del Instituto de Cultura Puertorriqueña* No. 65, 1974, 14-18. https://issuu.com/coleccionpuertorriquena/docs/primera_serie_n__mero_65 (accessed February 20, 2018).

called SEISES, in accordance with the cathedral at the hour of Vespers, a group of mulattos freely dancing various dances, without removing their hats, finding the manifestation of the Sacred Sacrament. In 1684, Bishop Fray Francisco de Padilla allowed these dances in the streets, and despite complaints, prohibited dancing in church.

> (En el Corpus (Christi) observábase en Puerto Rico la costumbre original de Sevilla, donde aún se practica por niños de coro que llaman SEISES, de concurrir a la catedral a la hora de vísperas, un grupo de mulatos libres a bailar varias danzas, sin quitarse los sombreros, hallándose de manifiesto el Santísimo Sacramento. En 1684 el obispo don Fray Francisco de Padilla hechó a la calle los danzantes, y aunque no faltaron quejas, el baile en la iglesia quedó suprimido.)[97]

Why, then, did the seis lose its significance as part of a Christian Catholic ritual and get replaced by a secular form? To answer this question, at least partially, one must return to the information presented by Cesáreo Rosa-Nieves and his investigation on the topic. Rosa-Nieves clearly illustrates to his readers that, in the eighteenth century, the Diocese of the Catholic Church was not pleased with the practice of incorporating the seis in sacred church practices. To clarify this sentiment, he cites the Spanish bishop Fray Pedro de Concepción y Urtiaga: "Some group members in the church appeared to appease the saints with a mass, wasting money from their organizations on dances, food, banquets. Overflowing with alcohol and sinful profanities." ("Los cofrades contentaban al santo con una misa, gastándose los dineros de la hermandad en bailes, comedias, banquetes. Corridas de cañas y profanidades pecaminosas."). [98]

---

[97] Salvador Brau, *Historia de Puerto Rico* (Nueva York, 1904), 158.
[98] Cesáreo Rosa-Nieves, "Los Bailes de Puerto Rico." *Revista del Instituto de Cultura Puertorriqueña* No. 65, 1974, 14-18.
https://issuu.com/coleccionpuertorriquena/docs/primera_serie_n__mero_65 (accessed February 20, 2018).

The Music of the Seis in Puerto Rico

Myriad studies have been written in relation to the musical context of the seis. Many of these sources from the end of the of the twentieth century and beginning of the twenty-first century focus from the perspective of the diversity and types of musical instruments used to perform the seis. Occasionally, musicologists and ethnomusicologists concentrate on the seis in relation to the *aguinaldo*: a type of folk music used frequently during the Christmas season.

It is important to clarify that the musical components of the seis do not consist solely of one genre or musical style. As part of an ethnographic study concerning the seis and its relation to música jíbara, Jaime Bofil Calero (2013) documents approximately more than ninety types of Puerto Rican seis. He divides these seis into rhythmic groups of duple meter and (in a smaller group) triple meter. Several of these seis had faded into obscurity by the time of his investigation.[99] According to his study, in which he cites Manuel Alonso and Antonio García de León respectively, Bofil mentions the Spanish fandango as the ancestor to the seis. Additionally, the seis began as a ternary form and gradually transformed into a binary form.[100]

One must comprehend how to differentiate aspects of the "seis as a dance" and the "seis as music." Also, it is indispensable and necessary to recognize the differences between the seis and the décima. The décima refers to the poetic structure that is usually accompanied by the music of the Puerto Rican seis through singing. To clarify this point, in his 1967 investigation on Puerto Rican folk music, Francisco López Cruz indicates that when people sing a series of decimas (regardless of topic)—the "seis fajardeño," for example—the generic name of the seis does not change.

---

[99] Jaime O. Bofil-Calero, "Capitulo 3: The Seis," in *Improvisation in Jíbaro Music: A Structural Analysis*, Tuscon, AZ: University of Arizona, 2013, 49, PhD Dissertation.

[100] Jaime O. Bofil-Calero, "Chapter 7: A Genealogy of the Seis," in *Improvisation in Jíbaro Music: A Structural Analysis*, Tuscon, AZ: University of Arizona, 2013, 137-198, PhD Dissertation; Manuel Alonso, "Escena V. Bailes de Puerto-Rico," in *El gíbaro: Cuadro de costumbres de la isla de Puerto-Rico* (Barcelona: D. Juan Oliveres, 1849) 55-68 (accessed April 14, 2015), Public Domain; Antonio García de León, *El mar de los deseos: El Caribe hispano musical, Historia y contrapunto* (México: Siglo Veintiuno Editores, 2002).

The trovador asks the musicians to play a seis fajardeño to sing based on any theme. People will still refer to this seis the seis fajardeño.[101]

Another significant point related to the seis and décima is that the "Seis con décima" ("Seis with Décima") forms an essential component of Puerto Rican folk music. Like many other seis, this uses the poetic structure of the décima in union with music. However, Francisco López Cruz mentions that people should not assume the belief that the "Seis con décima" functions as a style of folk music from Puerto Rico. Clearly, he indicates that the term "seis" is used when the singer of a slow seis uses the poetic schema named "décima" for the lyrics of the song. Many Puerto Rican musicians use the name "Seis con décima" to refer to a distinct melody of the seis.[102]

Musical Pentagram

Theoretical structures concerning musical aspects of the seis have been documented by different organizations like the Puerto Rican Cuatro Project, established in Connecticut in the 1990s, through easy methods where readers can also encounter information about the seis. Puerto Rican seis are versatile, can consist of characteristics from different geographical regions, dances or names of people: like the "Seis Andino" and musicians who became popular, like the "Seis Mapeye," "Seis Vallaran" and others.[103] The Puerto Rican seis uses both major and minor keys, depending on the type of seis performed. Thematic material for the seis when sung often presents diverse topics: pride in country, history, politics, and satire—

---

[101] Proyecto del Cuatro Puertorriqueño, "Nuestra Música Campesina: El Seis." http://www.cuatro-pr.org/es/node/179 (accessed January 23, 2018).

[102] Proyecto del Cuatro Puertorriqueño, http://www.cuatro-pr.org/es/node/179 (accessed January 23, 2018).

[103] Proyecto del Cuatro Puertorriqueño, http://www.cuatro-pr.org/es/node/179 (accessed Jauary 23, 2018); Conservatorio de Artes del Caribe. "Los estilos musicales folklóricos de Puerto Rico." 2014. http://www.artesdelcaribe.com/los-estilos-musicales-folkloricos-de-puerto-rico/ (accessed January 28, 2018).

usually, social commentary on the contemporary conditions on the island.[104]

In certain cases, as presented here in this study, several types of seis reflect the geography and dances from foreign regions of Latin American and other areas of the Caribbean (outside of Puerto Rico). Through my extensive research, I have encountered different types of Puerto Rican seis that reflect the geography, culture and music from Argentina. These seis also refer to both the creole gaucho culture and the cosmopolitan tango music.

---

[104] Manuel, Peter. "Puerto Rican Music and Cultural Identity: Creative Appropriation of Cuban Sources from Danza to Salsa," *Ethnomusicology* 38, No. 2 (1994). http://www.jstor.org/stable/851740 (accessed December 14, 2014).

"Ver para creer."
("See to believe.")

Musical Aspects of the Puerto Rican Seis: Analyses of Three Seis

To understand the musical aspect of the seis, one must dedicate some time to relating the music of the seis with Western music theory. In order to obtain this information, one must especially concentrate on rhythm, melody and harmonic analysis. This process occasionally involves comparing specific types of seis inspired by Argentine music (milonga, tango and music of the pampas).

Before proceeding, one must begin by talking about the methodological application used in this section. Analysis of Western music (from Europe and the United States) is based on the study of copies of scores in legible notation. On the other hand, the music of the Puerto Rican seis involves moments of much improvisation from musicians like the trovadors through the decima or decimilla.[105] It is common to interpret the musical piece, but nature of the music often does not feature a score and proves more complicated. Consider, for example, the collection of ethnographic recordings of cuatrististas interviewed by the Puerto Rican Cuatro Project. This organization has audio and transcriptions of conversations with musicians giving melodic examples and commentary. How many examples of "Seis Chorreao" are there? According to Efrain Vidal, one can take a slower genre and modify it as a "Seis Chorreao." For example, the "Seis Dorado" is a "Seis Chorreao" in a minor key.[106]

It is common for musical groups to create their own proper arrangements. Some musicians or experts in the field of Puerto Rican folk music, like Francisco López Cruz and Samuel Ramos, have written pedagogical books where they visually demonstrate how to play this music on folkloric instruments, like the Puerto Rican cuatro.[107] Music of seis written as scores in their original form are rare.

---

[105] Proyecto del Cuatro Puertorriqueño. "Nuestra Música Campesina: El Seis." http://www.cuatro-pr.org/es/node/179 (accessed January 23, 2018).

[106] Proyecto del Cuatro Puertorriqueño, "Nuestra Música Campesina: Muestra de 36 Distintos Seises y Aguinaldos." http://www.cuatro-pr.org/es/node/186 (accessed January 23, 2018).

[107] Francisco López Cruz, *Método para la enseñanza del cuatro puertorriqueño (Decimoquinta edición)*, (San Juan: PR: Fundación Francisco López Cruz, 2012); Samuel

The purpose behind the following musical analyses is not to concentrate on the improvisational sections of the seis. Jaime Bofil already conducted such an investigation concerning this type of Puerto Rican folk music in 2013. What matters in this section of the current study, besides demonstrating theoretical aspects of the music, is discussing the basic structures and sharing interesting or unusual musical aspects of each seis in question.

Rhythm

The seis often uses the simple duple meter of 2/4. Even though Puerto Rican folk music features different types of seis, this rhythmic meter appears in most versions. The seis uses patterns and rhythmic motives of the habanera, which originates from Cuban music. With this pattern, many musicologists like Luis Manuel Álvarez refer to the habanera as "café con pan." ("coffee with bread"). The reason for this phrase association stems from how the rhythm matches the words. This pattern frequently combines with other rhythmic motives, like the cinquillo (which contains five syncopated beats) and the "cha-chiqui-cha" rhythm (which refers to the sound of the güiro, or gourd, instrument).[108]

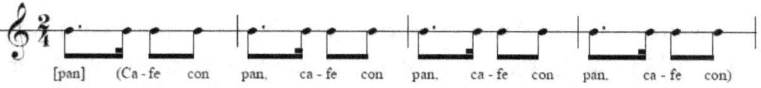

Example 1: Habanera Rhythm ("café con pan")

Ramos, *Los aguinaldos y seises para el cuatro puertorriqueño* (Book in English and Spanish) (Samuel Ramos, 2012); *Método de cuatro puertorriqueño, Vol. 1* (Samuel Ramos 2011).

[108] "Luis Manuel Álvarez explica la evolución de la música en Puerto Rico" (Extracto del documental *Salsa Opus 3* por Yves Billón de 1991, traducción en inglés), https://www.youtube.com/watch?v=EJ0RmsuKFHY&index=6&list=LL8mq JY4bOeb4IP285vKj4OA&t=0s (accessed February 8, 2018).

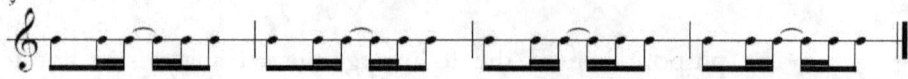

Example 2: Cinquillo Rhythm

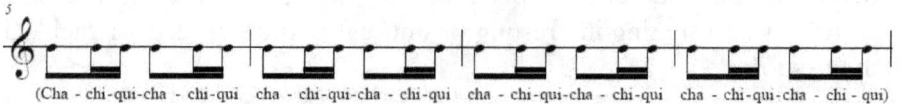

(Cha - chi-qui-cha - chi-qui   cha - chi-qui-cha - chi-qui   cha - chi-qui-cha - chi-qui   cha - chi-qui-cha - chi - qui)

Example 3: "Cha-chiqui-cha" Rhythm

The application of the habanera does not limit itself solely to the islands of Cuba or Puerto Rico. Different classical music composers from the Romantic era (c. 1825-1900) from Europe and the United States adopted the style of the habanera and the rhythm of the cinquillo to represent Spanish Exoticism. Musical exoticism attempts to depict foreign cultures and foreign music as something "unfamiliar" or "extravagant." One can detect the rhythmic pattern of the habanera in the opera *Carmen* (1875) by French composer Georges Bizet (1838-1875) and in the piano piece *Souvenir de Porto Rico: Marches des Gíbaros* (*Souvenir of Puerto Rico: March of the Mountain Men*) (1857) by the United States composer Louis Moreau Gottschalk (1829-1869).[109]

Regarding Latin America and the Caribbean, Álvarez notes that the habanera and cinquillo patterns manifest themselves in many other Latin American musical styles. He perceives this as the sharing or commonality among these distinct regions. While this music has different names and

---

[109] Georges Bizet, *Carmen* (Leipzig: C.F. Peters, 1920?), *IMSLP/Petrucci Biblioteca de Música*, http://imslp.org/wiki/Carmen_(Bizet,_Georges) (accessed February 12, 2018) Public Domain; Louis Moreau Gottschalk, *Souvenir de Porto Rico: Marche des Gíbaros*, IMSLP Petrucci, http://petrucci.mus.auth.gr/imglnks/usimg/0/08/IMSLP121790-SIBLEY1802.6864.7db0-39087012347029_Souvenir_P.pdf (accessed February 12, 2018) Public Domain.

styles, they are indirectly united through the habanera and cinquillo.¹¹⁰ In other words, they partake in a transcultural connection through the combination of cultural loss and gain. Applying this information to this study, Argentina is no exception. The habanera and cinquillo also appear in the milonga and tango.

New Musical Identity:
Melodic and Harmonic Analyses of Three Types of Puerto Rican Seis

Use of musical terminology, in relation to harmony, in many cases can convey different meanings. In other cases, different terms can give a concrete definition: one which can complicate finding and adding terns that can be used in a universal context. In part, the defect in the study of harmony is the inclination of using a strict formula with rules, norms, restrictions, and exceptions. In theoretical practice, there is the tendency to devise technical aspects, sometimes ignoring other musical elements.¹¹¹

In the 2010 study by Paloma Vidal and Claudia Púa Reyes, *La armonía en el tango. Un estudio desde el análisis armónico* (*Harmony in Tango. A Study of Harmonic Analysis*), they show the same rules or classical music theory and apply them to the popular music of Argentine tango. They devote their work to analyzing the harmonic elements of more than two-thousand five-hundred types of tangos. This form of analysis does not limit itself only to Latin American popular music. The same can apply to the Puerto Rican seis. In the attempt to locate the precise structure of the seis, specifically the universality of the seis, one must take into consideration that the music of the seis does not exist only in one format; as a result (as mentioned earlier), the content of melody changes depending on the type of seis performed. Recall also that the music of the seis presents sections with improvisation in the instrumental and sung sections with little or no written score used as a guide.

---

[110] "Luis Manuel Álvarez on the Evolution of Music in Puerto Rico" (Excerpt from the documentary *Salsa Opus 3* by Yves Billón de 1991, English Translation), https://www.youtube.com/watch?v=EJ0RmsuKFHY&index=6&list=LL8mqJY4bOeb4IP285vKj4OA&t=0s (accessed February 8, 2018).

[111] Paloma Vidal y Claudia Púa Reyes, *La armonía en el tango. Un estudio desde el análisis armónico*," (Santiago, CL: Universidad de Chile, 2010), 17, Seminario de Título Profesor Especializado en Teoría General de la Música.

Perhaps, the best approach to locating the melodic content is listening to the music. In this way, one can determine the direction of the melody because the vocal part from the trovador uses improvisation in décimas or decimillas. Concentrating on the instrumental melodic context that occurs before this section of the music works better. Why focus on that area? The beginning of the seis indicates to the listener and the public the type of seis being performed. In analyzing the melody from an aural perspective, consider these questions related to music theory and melodic structure:

1) Are there sections that contain conjunct, or connected, parts?
2) Does the melody feature disjunct parts, or sections separated by wide intervals?
3) Is there a combination of both elements in the melody?

When one hears Argentine folk music and Puerto Rican music inspired by this South American country, it is understood that they sound different. What matters is the transcultural element that combines the two cultures and, as a result, produces a new musical identity. The three types of seis analyzed here are Puerto Rican *interpretations* of Argentine musical styles. From a theoretical standpoint, one must look for similarities and differences in the melody and harmony regardless of how minute they may seem. One must always take into consideration that to analyze the melody, this process requires investigating where their recordings come from, given the fact that the same piece can have different interpretations.

Seis Milonga

To find the correct melody, or at least an approximation of it, one must carefully and relatedly listen to a recording and transcribe it based on aural memory. The tables presented at the end of this section are estimates of the harmonic structure based on musical recordings. It will not adhere to excessive analyses compared to the theoretical approach practice devised by Heinrich Schenker (1868-1935), which analyzes a tonal composition according to different levels of tonality.[112]

---

[112] Allen Cadwallader y David Gagne, *Analysis of Tonal Music: A Schenkerian Approach*, (New York: Oxford University Press, 2011).

Notice that in Table 3, the "Seis Milonga uses the key of g minor. Based on one recording, one can hear that the melody contains elements of both conjunct and disjunct segments. In relation to the harmonic structure of the "Seis Milonga," the majority of chord progressions are simple and logical with i-iv-V-I, like in measures 5 through 8. One curiosity occurs in measure 3 and 4. Even though the chords in this section form iv-i, some recordings suggest the presence of a secondary chord (0:00-0:07).[113]

If the milonga comes from Argentina, then why is this term incorporated as part of Puerto Rican folk music? This version of the milonga does not sound at all like the danceable milonga, which became the type which inspired the tango.[114] In the transcriptions of ethnographic interviews from the Puerto Rican Cuatro Project, the musicians who play these seis do not explain this connection. They only mention how to play them and the key of the piece.[115]

The type of milonga used in the "Seis Milonga" from Puerto Rico refers to the milonga campera. The seis milonga and seis milonguero are some of the most influential styles in Puerto Rico. Even though these styles were created by musicians from the island, one can observe the rhythmic characteristics of the habanera, partaking in the African races. The genre of the seis from the twentieth century resulted from the participation from Puerto Rican trovadors attending international festivals outside the island, where they began incorporating musical styles from other countries like the arpeggiated pattern of the milonga in the payada.[116]

Seis Tango

Comparing the "Seis Milonga" with the "Seis Tango," this last type uses a major key. In certain cases, the "Seis Tango" consists of a major key

---

[113] Saborboricuapr1, "Seis Milonga Instrumental (Cuatro Puertorriqueño),"
https://www.youtube.com/watch?v=2KiavRgeV80 (accessed April 16, 2018).

[114] Very Tango Store, "La historia de la milonga,"
https://www.verytangostore.com/tango-milonga.html (accessed February 12, 2018).

[115] Proyecto del cuatro Puertorriqueño, "Nuestra Música Campesina: Muestra de 36 Distintos Seises y Aguinaldos." http://www.cuatro-pr.org/es/node/186 (accessed January 23, de 2018).

[116] Jaime O. Bofil-Calero, "Capitulo 3: El Seis," en *La improvisación en la música jíbara: Un análisis de la estructura* (Tuscon, AZ: Universidad de Arizona, 2013), 65-66, Disertación Doctoral de filosofía.

of G Major or C Major. Also, the melody of the "Seis Tango" from measures 6 through 16 features nearly the same descending direction, like the "Seis Milonga": with the difference of parallel keys. In addition to this, like in the "Seis Milonga," the melody of the "Seis Tango" also contains a combination of conjunct and disjunct sections. The harmonic progression in the "Seis Tango" also contains secondary dominant chords. In this case, a V/V7 chord appears in measure 2 and a V7/V in measure 5. Also, other secondary harmonies of V6/ii manifest themselves in measures 9 and 13.[117]

Seis Pampero

The "Seis Pampero" has several similarities with the "Seis Tango" in relation to the use of a major key and the direction of the melody. The "Seis Pampero" uses the key of D Major and contains a combination of both conjunct and disjunct fragments in the melodic construction. The chords in its harmonic structure are easy to locate and analyze because they repeat frequently throughout most of the musical piece (IV-I-V-I).[118] In addition to the simplicity of this progression, compared to the complexity of the "Seis Milonga," it is important to notice a significant difference in the "Seis Pampero." This seis does not feature secondary dominant chords. Except for the IV6 chord in measures 6 and 14, most of the chords are in root position.

---

[117] Orquesta de San Sebastián, "Seis Tango," https://www.youtube.com/watch?v=4rYYWjOXO1g (accessed February 8, 2018).

[118] Jann Rodri. "Puerto Rico se levanta seis pampero (cosas buenas sacaré)," https://www.youtube.com/watch?v=VvpNZk43Ghw (accessed February 8, 2018).

Table 3: Structure of the "Seis Milonga"

Key	Measures	Harmonic Progression
g minor	1-4	i—iv—(iv)—I
	5-8	i—iv—V—i
	9-12	i—V—(V)—i
	13-16	i—V—(V)—i

Table 5: Structure of the "Seis Tango"

Key	Measures	Harmonic Progression
C Major (or G Major)	1-4	I—V/V7—V7—I
	5-8	V7/V—V/V—V7—I
	9-12	I—V6/ii—ii—V—I
	13-16	I—V6/ii—ii—V—I

Table 6: Structure of the "Seis Pampero"

Key	Measures	Harmonic Progression
D Major	1-4	IV—I—V—I
	5-8	IV—I—IV6—V—I
	9-12	IV—I—V—I
	13-16	IV—I—IV6—V—I

"El que pregunta no yerra."

("He who asks does not err.")

The Tango Canción

How does one define the *tango canción* ("tango song")? It is a lyrical musical composition where the words correspond to the emotional and rhythmic characteristics of the music and dance. Concerning the history of this musical form, the first interpreter of this genre was a singer of música campera and payadas named Carlos Gardel. The musical piece "Mi noche triste" ("My Sad Night") was written by Samuel Castriota and Pasqual Contursi. Even though they created this piece in 1916, its public premiere occurred the following year. The tango canción celebrated its centennial in 2017.[119] The theme for "Mi noche triste" is a monologue about a man lamenting being abandoned by the woman he loves. The tango cancion can also be defined as a "complaint" or "lament."[120]

With the tango canción, a new movement emerged where composers and arrangers could express their sentiments about love, patriotism and social consciousness: as was the case with the tango "Cambalache," previously mentioned as an example of censorship in radio broadcasts. Composer and actor Enrique Santos Discépolo wrote this tango in 1934.[121] "Cambalache" forms part of the most recognized tango songs of the era and in contemporary times. Discépolo composed this tango for the film *El alma del bandoneón* (*The Soul of the Bandoneon*), which premiered in 1936. The definition of the word "cambalache" refers to a second-hand store in Buenos Aires. Scholars like Gregorio Selser indicate that Discépolo uses this term as a metaphor for the terrible socioeconomic conditions in Argentina in the "Infamous Decade."[122]

---

[119] El observador: "Mi noche triste." "Cien años atrás, Gardel estrenaba el primer tango canción de la historia," *Perfil,* http://www.perfil.com/elobservador/cien-anos-atras-gardel-estrenaba-el-primer-tango-cancion-de-la-historia.phtml, el 7 de enero de 2017 (accessed April 13, 2018).

[120] Fernanda Jara, "Cumple 100 anos "Mi noche triste", el primer tango canción grabado por Gardel," *Infobae,* https://www.infobae.com/cultura/2017/06/11/cumple-100-anos-mi-noche-triste-el-primer-tango-cancion-grabado-por-gardel/ (accessed April 13, 2018).

[121] Some scholars suggest that Enrique Santos Discépolo wrote this song one year later.

[122] Gregorio Selser, "Prohíbese el tango 'Cambalache,' escrito en 1935. Molesto espejo." *El Dia,* 26 de octubre de 1981, 55.; Enrique Santos Discépolo, "Cambalache," *Enrique Santos Discépolo "El poeta del tango"*—*Bs As Tango* [Buenos Aires (¿?): El Bandoneón, 2010], 2.

Analyzing "Cambalache" (See Table 6), one can see that this tango canción uses the key of D Major. Most of the harmony in this composition also contains logical progressions like I-V-I, IV-I and ii-V-I; this last progression is frequently encountered in jazz music. However, there are several sections of "Cambalache" that that have secondary chords, like in measure 16 and measures 19 to 20. Even though a secondary chord appears there, it can function as a type of V/iv o V/ii. Listening to this song and the lyrics again, specifically from 0:47 to 0:54 up to the word "traidor" ("traitor"), the music resolves on a chord of ii. Also, it is possible that this moment of confusion in the harmonic progression reflects the same sentiment of confusion of Argentine society in the 1930s.[123]

Table 6: "Cambalache," Harmonic Analysis

Key	Verses	Measures	Harmonic Progression[124]
D Major	First Verse, Second Verse	1-4	I—V—ii(V)—vii°—I
		5-8	I—V—ii(V)—V—I
		9-12	IV(iv)—I—ii—V—I
		13-16	IV(iv)—I—ii—V—I—V/V—V
		17-20	I—V7/IV—IV—V6/5/ii—ii—vi (?)
		21-24	ii—V—I—V—I—ii(?)—I6—V
		25-28	V7—I—V—I—ii(?)—I6—V
		29-32	ii—V—I—V—I—V7—IV—I
		33-37	IV—V—I—V—I—V—I

---

[123] Enrique Santos Discépolo, "Cambalache," *Enrique Santos Discépolo "El poeta del tango"*—*Bs As Tango* [Buenos Aires (¿?): El Bandoneón, 2010], 2. This audio recording is performed in the key of C Major and not the original key.

[124] The analysis presented in this table is my interpretation, based on the octaves of the harmony. It does not suggest that this is the only way to analyze the harmony.

"Al buen entendedor con pocas palabras vasta."
("Few words are enough for the one who understands well.")

The Décima: Reevaluating its Structure and Performance

The décima constitutes an archaic poetic form created in Spain in the Colonial times known as the "décima espinela." In the 2015 study by Maximiano Trapero entitled, *El origen y triunfo de la décima: Revisión de un tópico de cuatro siglos y noticias de nuevas, primeras e inéditas décimas*[125], the author uncovers more details concerning its origin. He says that, through scientific certainty, it is understood that Don Vicente Espinel did not create the décima "espinela." The declaration that Vicente Espinel devised this poetic form was propagated in 1923 by the Spanish historian Rodríguez Marín.[126]

The problems that Trapero has with this statement from Rodríguez Marín are that Marín does not supply credible evidence to confirm that Vicente Espinel wrote the first décima. In addition to this error, none of the historians from the past who talk about the décima mention Marín nor his contributions.[127] Trapero also warns readers that is also incorrect to apply the term "décima espinela" to classify a décima. Citing Marín, again, Trapero indicates that the décima "espinela" was used as a poetic term in the seventeenth century: one-hundred years *after* the life of Espinel.[128] However, Trapero alludes that the contribution from Espinel stems from the accomplishment that the stanza of ten octosyllabic verses acquired its mature and expressive metrics, to fix the definitive form through the combination of rhymes and to intertwine these verses in a closed form. Because of this, the décima quickly reached popularity. His

---

[125] In English, the title roughly translates to, *The Origin and Triumph of the Décima: Revision of a Topic from Four Centuries and Updates of New, First and Unedited Décimas*

[126] Maximiano Trapero, "Capítulo I: Vicente Espinel y la décima espinela: 1, El elogio de la décima," en *El origen y triunfo de la décima: Revisión de un tópico de cuatro siglos y noticias de nuevas, primeras e inéditas decimas* (Valencia: Publicaciones de la Universidad de Valencia, 2015), 21-27.

[127] Maximiano Trapero, "Capítulo I: Vicente Espinel y la décima espinela: 1, El elogio de la décima," en *El origen y triunfo de la décima: Revisión de un tópico de cuatro siglos y noticias de nuevas, primeras e inéditas decimas* (Valencia: Publicaciones de la Universidad de Valencia, 2015), 21-27.

[128] Maximiano Trapero, "Capitulo 2: Las palabras *decima* y *espinela*," en *El origen y triunfo de la décima: Revisión de un tópico de cuatro siglos y noticias de nuevas, primeras e inéditas decimas* (Valencia: Publicaciones de la Universidad de Valencia, 2015), 28-58.

décima changed into the octosyllabic stanza mostly practiced in the seventeenth century: as a long sonnet and the short verse of the décima "espinela."[129]

Maximiano Trapero mentions that the structure of a décima consists of the form "abbaaccddc." This form should have eight syllables for every line in order to create eight octosyllables. Trapero explains the belief that a décima has two connected stanzas of five lines each. He uses the book *Métrica española (Spanish Metrics)* by Navarro Tomás to justify that a décima really contains two stanzas of four lines each: the first through fourth line as "abba" and the seventh through final line as "cddc." Additionally, these two lines are connected by the fifth and sixth lines "ac."[130] Continuing with this topic, included here are different tables (Tables 7 through 9) with precise explanations of the terms and concepts of poetic structure, forms of stanzas and the general structure of the décima.[131]

Table 7: Concepts of Poetic Structure

Meter	Literary science that concerns the rhythmic conformation of linguistic context
Poem	Set of verses that constitute a work of art, an expressive form by its creator
Stanza	A set of two or more verses which have assonant or consonant rhyme, distributed in a fixed way

---

[129] Maximiano Trapero, "Capítulo 1: Vicente Espinel y la décima espinela: 1, El elogio de la décima," en *El origen y triunfo de la décima: Revisión de un tópico de cuatro siglos y noticias de nuevas, primeras e inéditas decimas* (Valencia: Publicaciones de la Universidad de Valencia, 2015), 21-27

[130] Maximiano Trapero, "Capitulo 2: Las palabras *decima* y *espinela*," en *El origen y triunfo de la décima: Revisión de un tópico de cuatro siglos y noticias de nuevas, primeras e inéditas decimas* (Valencia: Publicaciones de la Universidad de Valencia, 2015), 28-58; Tomás Navarro Tomás, *Métrica española: Reseña histórica y descriptiva* (Madrid: Ediciones Guadarrama, 1972), 268-269.

[131] Antonio Quilis, *La métrica española* (Madrid: Ediciones Alcalá, 1975), https://treseso.files.wordpress.com/2009/05/la-metrica-espanola.pdf (accessed April 6, 2018).

Verse	The smallest unit, the minor structural division encountered in a poem. Should exist only when found in use of another verse forming part of the stanza and, afterwards, part of the poem
Rhyme	The (total or partial) acoustic identity between two or more verses of situated sounds starting at the last sharp vowels.
Consonant Rhyme	The reiteration, in two or more verses, of vowels and consonants found at the beginning of the last sharp vowel
Assonant Rhyme	The reiteration, in two or more verses, of vowels found at the beginning of the last sharp vowel

Table 8: Stanza Forms

2 Verses	**Pareado (Pair)**	Important that it has only one rhyme
3 Verses	**Terceto (Third)**	3 verses of *Arte Mayor*[132], rhyme ABA-BCB-CDC…
4 Verses	**Cuarteto (Fourth)**	Arte Mayor, ABBA
		Redondilla, *arte menor*[133] 8 syllables, abba
		Cuarteta, like the redondilla, but abab…
Paired	**Serventesio**	Arte Mayor, 7-5-7-5, assonant rhyme in paired verses
5 Verses	**Quinteto (Fifth)**	Arte Mayor, different rhyming combinations
	Quintilla (Smaller Version of Fifth)	Arte menor
	Lira	Alternating verse, 7-11-7-7-11, aBabB
6 Verses	**Sexteto (Sixth)**	7-11-7-11-7-11, aBaBcC…
	Sextilla (Smaller Version of Sixth)	Arte menor, different rhyming combinations

---

[132] Arte Mayor contains nine to eleven syllables
[133] Arte menor contains eight syllables or less.

	Sexta rima (Another Version of Sixth)	Arte Mayor, 11 syllables, ABABCC…
7 Verses	Seguidilla	Arte menor, 7-5-7-5-5-7-5, no fixed rhyme
8 Verses	Octava (Eighth)	Arte Mayor, 11 syllables, ABABABCC
10 Verses	Décima (Tenth)	Arte menor, 8 syllables, abbaaccddc

Table 9: General Structure of the Décima

Poetic Structure and Rhyme	Number of Line in the Décima	Description
a	1	The first line of improvised text
b	2	A new line of improvised text
b	3	The same rhyme scheme as the 2nd line
a	4	The same rhyme scheme as the 1st line
a	5	The same rhyme scheme as the 4th line of text
c	6	A new line of improvised text
c	7	The same rhyme scheme as the 6th line of text
d	8	A new line of improvised text
d	9	The same rhyme scheme as the 8th line of text
c	10	The same rhyme scheme as the 6th and 7th lines of text

"A quien amasa y cuece, muchas cosas le acontecen."
("Anything that can happen will happen to bakers and cooks.")

The Origin and Structure of the Argentine Payada

"Everyone take care of their own which is the most direct thing to not abandon your harvest, which the gaucho has grown." —Estanislao del Campo

("Cuide cada uno lo suyo que es la cosa más derecha no abandone su cosecha, el gaucho que haiga sembrao."—Estanislao del Campo

Historian Matías Isolabella defines the payada rioplatense as a performative genre based on the traditions of improvised poetry and song. Its history is documented along diverse cultures. The characteristics and origin of this artistic expression maintain a long relation with the Ibero-American traditions; the payador is considered related to the Medieval European juglar—trovador, trouvère, Meistersinger, etc. The principal role between two or more improvisators is the poetic duel.[134]

It deserves mention that, in his description of the payada, Isolabella indicates poetic and syllabic characteristics that define the Spanish décima "espinela": characteristics, which could apply to the rustic version of the Puerto Rican décima through improvisation. In relation to the history of the payada, he says that the décima "espinela" was used in Argentina as a poetic base in the 1700s and popularized in that country in the 1800s. The author attributes the popularization of the payada in Argentina to the payador Gabino Ezeiza. Towards the end of the nineteenth century, the payada began to assume the characteristics of its true form.[135]

The payador Gabino Ezeiza, one of the most important figures of that generation, is credited for introducing songs for milonga and the popularization of the genre in urban contexts. His payada became etched in history as the first true payada of the rioplatense, when the Argentine improvisator confronted Juan de Nava (1856-1919) on July 23, 1884 in a challenge still remembered today. The payadores are also known with

---

[134] Matías N. Isolabella, "Estructuras de improvisación en la payada rioplatense: definición y análisis." *Revista Argentina de Musicología* 12-13 (2012), 151-182.
[135] Matías N. Isolabella, 151-182.

different names in some parts of the world: in Latin America, they are "cantores repentistas," from Brazil the "cangaçeiros" singers; from Cuba "punto guajiro," from Venezuela and Costa Rica the "repentistas llaneros, and "trovador" in Spain and Puerto Rico.[136]

The principal structure of the milonga consists of eight metric subdivisions, grouped into four in the binary metric unit, but implicitly accented in the first, fourth and seventh subdivision. It features the rhythmic schema of "3-3-2," which is greatly extended in America. The milonga supports variants of sensible differences, from the aggressive and stinging accentuation of the milonga oriental to the lyrical and tender milonga campera. Adding variations from the past includes two types of equal denomination, distinct intention and "tempo" as can be encountered in the tango. Musicologists have debated the origin of the milonga without concentrating much on its continental validity; they focus more on area where a strong migratory presence exists.[137]

Like other historians from the past, Matías Isolabella proposes that Don Vicente Espinel created the la décima (or décima espinela). Although it is already understood that this information is incorrect, one must remember that Isolabella conducted his investigation in 2012: three years *before* the critical study prepared by Maximiano Trapero. One should not compare nor criticize the work and investigative study by Isolabella, which by that time consisted of contemporary and precise information.

---

[136] Matías N. Isolabella, 151-182.

[137] Ana María Romanuik, "Hacia la búsqueda de la particularidad de 'modelo de hacer' de la música y los músicos pampeanos," *Sociedad Argentina para las Ciencias Cognitivas de la Música (SACCoM)*, 2011; Daniel Martin Duarte Loza, "Una poética pampa. Integración cultural entre Brasil, Argentina y Uruguay: música, clima, historia, y Geografía," *AURA. Revista de Historia y Teoría del Arte* No. 3 (2015), 17-37.

Table 10: Examples of the Argentine Payada Puerto Rican Décima

Argentine Payada	Puerto Rican Decima
Third Stanza of the Epic Payada, Santos Vega	*First Stanza of the Décima about the Puerto Rican Cuatro*
They say that, on a cloudy night,	Here is made an instrument
if (with) his guitar some young man	From the trunk of a guaraguao (tree)
by the crest of a lake	Played on it is a seis chorreao
leaves the intent hanging,	A talented musician
the shadow comes unannounced	The Aguinaldo laments
and, upon being enveloped in her cloak,	The Cayeyano, Cagueño
sounds the prelude to a song	Milonga, Seis Fajardeño
between the dormant strings,	The Danza, as well as a Danzón.
strings that vibrate wounded	All have been interpreted with
as if from tears.	The Puerto Rican cuatro.
(Dicen que, en noche nublada,	(Aquí se hace un instrumento
si su guitarra algún mozo	Del tronco de un guaraguao
en el crucero del pozo	Toca en el un seis chorreao
deja de intento colgada,	Un musico de talento.
llega la sombra callada	El aguinaldo lamento
y, al envolverla en su manto,	El cayeyano, cagueño
suena el preludio de un canto	Milonga, seis fajardeño
entre las cuerdas dormidas,	La danza igual que un danzón.
cuerdas que vibran heridas	Todos se interpretan con
como por gotas de llanto.)[138]	El cuatro puertorriqueño.)[139]

Comparisons Between the Argentine Payada and the Puerto Rican Seis

The payada, shown on the left, was written by the Argentine poet Rafael Obligado (1851-1920). It tells the romanticized folktale about the life and works of one of the first gauchos and payadors from Argentina. The life of Santos Vega is shrouded in mystery. Although he was a real

---

[138] Payadas, "Santos Vega El alma del payador," http://payadas.com/santos-vega-el-alma-de-payador (accessed March 5, 2018).
[139] Luis Miranda (Transcrita por David Morales), "El cuatro puertorriqueño," en Proyecto del Cuatro Puertorriqueño, "Decimas inspiradas por el cuatro puertorriqueño," http://www.cuatro-pr.org/es/node/171 (accessed March 5, 2018).

person who participated in challenges, ending his career after losing to the Chilean payador Juan Gualberto Godoy, sources mention that some contemporary authors preferred to exaggerate the portrayal of Godoy in this episode by comparing him to the Devil.[140]

This work serves multiple purposes. Notice that the structure of a payada is identical to that of the Puerto Rican décima. Comparing the two structures, I have included one stanza of the payada. On the right is a stanza of a Puerto Rican décima by Luis Miranda about the theme of the folkloric instrument of the cuatro. Both consist of ten lines per stanza, usually with each line an octosyllable. They also use the same rhyming structure at the end of each line: "abbaaccddc." Like the Argentine payadas, the Puerto Rican decima uses as its poetic inspiration themes related to farming life, history, patriotism, nature, and social commentary among others.

In the same manner as the Puerto Rican décima, the lyrics to a payada are improvised. Depending on how it is performed, payadas can have music or solely spoken poetry. According to Matías Isolabella, the song respects the rhythmic accentuation and, to some extent, is improvised. The improvisation is *subconscious*, and the payadores do not think about which motes to sing, but about which words to pronounce. Concepts are organized in pairs of octosyllabic verses which correspond to two beats. Singing is in syllabic style and develops a melodic profile descended from degrees of groups. As happens with the abilities of the guitarist, talents vary according to personal circumstances.[141] In the following table, I give a small explanation about what constitutes a syllable and how to count them in a décima.

---

[140] Payadas, "Santos Vega El alma del payador," http://payadas.com/santos-vega-el-alma-de-payador (accessed March 5, 2018).

[141] Matías N. Isolabella, "Estructuras de improvisación en la payada rioplatense: definición y análisis." *Revista Argentina de Musicología* 12-13 (2012), 151-182.

Table 11: Rules for Rhymes in a Puerto Rican Décima

Verse or line ending with a word stressed on the **last syllable**	The total number of syllables in the verse should be eight syllables.
When ending with a word stressed on the **last syllable**	Add one syllable to the total number of syllables.
Verse ending on a word stressed on the **third-to-last syllable**	Subtract one syllable from the total number of syllables.
Synaloepha	When the verse ends on a vowel and the next one on a word that begins on a vowel, two syllables count as one.
Hiatus	Vowel *i, u* together with vowel *a, o, e*, the accent goes on the weak vowel.

Musical Instruments and Elements

Musical instruments for a décima can consist of chordophones like guitars, cuatros, tiple, bordonua, and other percussion instruments like güiro, claves or bongo.[142] For the payada, the instrumentation is simple: guitar and voice. The melody in a Puerto Rican seis appears almost immediately at the beginning of the musical piece, which defines the type of seis. The melody in a payada does not appear until the improvised section from the payador, as in the piece "Tata Quiero Ser Diputado" ("I Want to Be a Deputy") by Gustavo Guichón (0:00-0:09, 0:09-0:32). A payada begins with arpeggiated chords.[143]

The payada uses a basic harmonic structure: usually, a progression of the chords i-iv-V in minor keys, or I-IV-V in major keys and constantly repeated. Recall that the harmonic progressions in Puerto Rican seis differ depending on the type of seis. They use, in some cases, secondary and complex chords. The decimas form part of the Puerto Rican folk music. Payadas are part of the folk music of the gauchos from Argentina and other

---

[142] Proyecto del Cuatro Puertorriqueño, "Nuestra Música Campesina: El Seis," http://www.cuatro-pr.org/es/node/179 (accessed January 23, 2018).

[143] "Payada del campo argentino," https://www.youtube.com/watch?v=DaifV8QFUb0&t=117s (accessed March 13, 2018).

South American countries. In relation to the performance of a payada, Matías Isolabella says that for the payadors, the arpeggio of the milonga represents a mechanical and repetitive gesture that does not require much attention during presentation. He suggests that, even though the guitar can function as part of a payada, this instrument does not function as the focus of this genre of folk music. Guitarists strive to be experts in the use of their instrument, and those who do not dominate it constantly preoccupy themselves with fine tuning the instrument. Every improvisator has their original approach to arpeggiation.[144]

Puerto Rican "Controversias" and Argentine "Contrapuntos"

In this section, it is important to mention a subgenre present in both styles of music with different names: *controversia* (*controversy*) and *contrapunto* (counterpoint[145]). In Puerto Rico, the controversia is a type of competitive décima between two people over a prescribed theme. The objective of a controversia is to demonstrate the improvisational skills of each trovador. The trovadors can improvise one after the other. However, there are moments when a trovador can use repetition to stress several lines, or they can interrupt the other trovador by creating a new décima.[146]

The contrapunto from Argentina functions in the same way as the Puerto Rican controversia. Contrapuntos consist of two payadors singing or speaking over a theme, and the payadors must improvise.[147] Like the Puerto Rican controversia, it is important that each payador is dexterous

---

[144] Matías N. Isolabella, "Estructuras de improvisación en la payada rioplatense: definición y análisis." *Revista Argentina de Musicología* 12-13 (2012), 151-182.

[145] To clarify, the term "counterpoint" in this context does not refer to the "note against note" definition frequently used to describe compositional aspects of Western classical music from the Baroque and Classical eras.

[146] Peter Manuel, "Puerto Rican Music and Cultural Identity: Creative Appropriation of Cuban Sources from Danza to Salsa," *Etnomusicology* 38, No. 2 (1994). http://www.jstor.org/stable/851740 (accessed December 14, 2014); Consuelo Posada, "La décima cantada en el Caribe y la fuerza de los procesos de identidad." *Revista de Literaturas Populares*, 3, No. 2 (2003). 141-154 (accessed January 19, 2018).

[147] Ana María Romanuik, "Hacia la búsqueda de la particularidad de 'modelo de hacer' de la música y los músicos pampeanos," *Sociedad Argentina para las Ciencias Cognitivas de la Música (SACCoM)*, 2011.

in improvisation.[148] Earlier in this study, I discussed the fame of the payador Gabino Ezeiza and his participation in the first publicized payada competition against Pablo Vázquez. The rules for this competition from 1894 were created for the public interested in participating. According to one report from the era, these were some of the written rules. They mentioned the date and location of the performance, designation of judges, determination of the prize, and designation of the theme for the contrapunto. These rules also prohibited competitors from plagiarizing verses or threatening physical harm against each other; they also explained the designation (by draw) of the first payador who begins to sing and the election and submission of the themes of the contrapunto to the representatives of each payador.[149]

Preserving the Art of Improvisation

To promote the conservation of the Puerto Rican décima and Argentine payada as exponents of creole races, governmental agencies like the Institute of Puerto Rican Culture (Instituto de Cultura Puertorriqueña) and groups like the Santovegano National Encounter of Payadors (Encuentro Nacional Santovegano de Payadors) among many others have dedicated time and effort to establishing educational programs and annual festivals to create interest and new generations of trovadores. In Puerto Rico, trovador competitions have been celebrated on the island for more than fifty years. The first regional competitions began its celebration in 1957. Some notable festivals worthy of mention are the Festival of Trovadores in the city of Ponce in honor of Juan Antonio Romero and "The Ramito Vive Festival" in Caguas. It was not until 1969 that groups organized competitions and "Semi-Finals." Puerto Rico alone has more than seventy *trova* festivals.[150]

With the existence of a grand number of groups of trovadores on the island, it is common to have festivals of different categories in multiple regions at the same time. It is worth indicating that awards for these

---

[148] Matías N. Isolabella, "Estructuras de improvisación en la payada rioplatense: definición y análisis." *Revista Argentina de Musicología* 12-13 (2012), 151-182.
[149] Matias N. Isolabella, 151-182.
[150] Decimania, "La Semana del Trovador Puertorriqueño," http://www.decimania.com/index.php/semana-del-trovador (accessed April 10, 2018).

competitions come in the form of monetary prizes. By 2018, in light of socioeconomic crises and hurricanes on the island, these awards have become difficult to maintain. One of the challenges for trovadors in this era stems from mastering the décima "espinela," which must use perfect rhyme. The verse provided to improvise and write must be from memory. The entire verse must be sung and completed in less than two minutes.[151] Trovadors who have surpassed these categories in other decades are known as "The King of Trovadors" (German Rosario), "Golden Beak" (Luis Miranda Fernández) and "The Excellent Espinelista" (Mariano Cotto).

The celebration of the of the payador serves as an homage to the first challenge of Gabino Ezeiza in Montevideo (in Uruguay). Like in Puerto Rico, in South America there are communities and groups who work arduously in the preservation, tradition and legacy of the payadas and their interpreters. Here are several celebrations and competitions about payadas: July 23 in Argentina, August 23 in Uruguay and June 24 in Chile. The Santovegano Encounter of Payadors in San Clemente Tuyu has held celebrations for the past thirty-six years. The 2017 celebration included two nights of song and poetry from different points of the province of Bueno Aires, with outstanding payadors like Omar Moreno Palacios, Luis Genaro and Luis Avello to name a few. The Encounter of Payadors in Chile has been celebrated for the past twenty-five years, where Pedro Yánez won the first President Award and Altazor Award. Today, the tradition and cultivation of the art of improvisation continues. For example, in 2018, Encounters of Payadors from Salliquelo in Bueno Aires celebrated their third year of challenges.[152]

---

[151] Decimania, http://www.decimania.com/index.php/semana-del-trovador (accessed April 10, 2018); Jaime Torres Torres, "Roberto Silva, nuevo trovador nacional." *Fundación Nacional para la Cultura Popular*, el 20 de noviembre de 2015, https://prpop.org/2015/11/roberto-silva-nuevo-trovador-nacional/ (accessed April 10, 2018); Joan Gross, "'Defendiendo la (Agri)Cultura: Reterritorializing Culture in the Puerto Rican Décima," *Oral Tradition* 23, Iss. 2 (2008). 219-234.

[152] "Encuentro Santosvegano de Payadores de San Clemente 2017," *Televisión Pública Argentina*, http://www.tvpublica.com.ar/programa/36-encuentro-santosvegano-de-payadores-de-san-clemente-2017/ (accessed April 9, 2018).

"Amistades que son ciertas mantienen las puertas abiertas."

("True friends leave their doors open.")

Conclusion

With gratefulness I recall the words from one of my professors when they referred to the objective of history: "The point of history is not to uncover the truth about what happened, but to uncover what is beautiful." Resources of information change constantly, no matter if viewed from a historical or musicological standpoint. What signifies that something was correct yesterday, the same could be refuted tomorrow.

In the study of music, scholars and specialists pay special attention to the true interpreters of oral tradition, where these have been recorded and cataloged as folkloric genres for future generations. For some, the circumstances of these investigations can prove receptive. Bruno Nettl suggests applying the following approach; making an inventory of one musical culture can produce an inventory of concepts and categories which society uses in their musical culture as basic material taken from their terminology or concepts.[153]

This study has taken into consideration the use of the terms "ethnocentric perspective" and "cultural appropriation." The first term can illicit erroneous and negative interpretations about a culture by implying the superiority of one culture over another. Cultural appropriation for personal use implies stealing from foreign cultural identities for personal gain and not acknowledging the original cultures in question. Throughout this study, I have tried diligently to not commit these mistakes. However, it is unavoidable to objectively represent all cultures without expressing some bias. As a basic rule, one should always maintain a level of respect toward a different culture. However, there will always be groups that do not accept the ideas presented.[154]

---

[153] Bruno Nettl. "11: You Will Never Understand This Music: Insiders and Outsiders," in *The Study of Ethnomusicology: Thirty-Three Discussions* (Urbana, IL: University of Illinois Press, 2015), 157-68.

[154] Bruno Nettl, 157-168.

The information illustrated in this book does not present an apologetic depiction of two cultures. I have tried to present a transparent panorama of the musical history of the jíbaro and the gaucho. The legacy of the jíbaro and gaucho today is due, thanks to the thousands of countrymen who live day to day for a miserable wage so that others can enjoy their coffee or mate and the technology of the times.

Appendix:
Table of Folk Music from Puerto Rico and Argentina

County/Territory	Puerto Rico	Argentina
Name	Seis	Payada
Musical Genre	Música folklórica (*música jíbara*)	Música campera (*música gaucha*)
Structure	Ten lines of text—each line an *octosyllable* (eight syllables per line)	Ten lines of text—each line an *octosyllable* (eight syllables per line)
Types	Varies by different regions of Puerto Rico—consist of: Names of cities or towns in Puerto Rico People Dances/popular music from other parts of Latin America or Europe Major or minor keys Voice—solo, or between two people (*controversias*)	Varies by countries of Argentina, Uruguay, Chile y Paraguay Voice— solo, or between two people (*contrapunto*)
Musical Instruments	Puerto Rican cuatros, tiple, bordonúa, guitar, percussion, voice	Guitar(s) and voices
Themes	Love Home Life/Society Puerto Rican Geography Religion (especially during Christmas or other sacred Christian events) Politics/Comedy	Love Home Life/Society Argentine Geography Politics/Comedy

Works Cited

Bibliography

Alonso, Manuel. *El gibaro: Cuadro de costumbres de la isla de Puerto-Rico* (Barcelona: D. Juan Oliveres, 1849). Accessed April 14, 2015.

Arapoglou, Eleftheria: Monika Fodor and Jopi Nyman. *Mobile Narratives: Travel, Migration, and Transculturation.* New York: Routledge, 2013.

Arguedas, José María. *Formación de una cultura nacional Indoamericana.* Coyoacán, MX: Siglo veintiuno editores, 1975, 1998.

Atiles, Francisco del Valle. *El campesino puertorriqueño: sus condiciones físicas, intelectuales y morales, causas que las determinan y medios para mejorarlas.* San Juan: Tipo de Gonzales Font, 1889). https://freeditorial.com/es/books/el-campesino-puertorriqueno-sus-condiciones-fisicas-intelectuales-y-morales. Accessed February 4, 2018.

Benedetti, Héctor. *Nueva historia del tango: De los orígenes al siglo XXI.* Buenos Aires: Siglo XXI Editores, 2015.

Benítez-Rojo, Antonio and James E. Maraniss (English Trans.). *The Repeating Island: The Caribbean and the Postmodern Perspective, Second Edition.* Durham, NC: Duke University Press, 1997.

Bizet, Georges. *Carmen* (Leipzig: C.F. Peters, 1920?), Public Domain, *IMSLP/Petrucci Music Library*, http://imslp.org/wiki/Carmen_(Bizet,_Georges). Accessed February 12, 2018.

Bofil-Calero, Jaime O. *Improvisation in Jíbaro Music: A Structural Analysis.* Tuscon, AZ: University of Arizona, 2013. PhD Dissertation.

Brau, Salvador. *Historia de Puerto Rico.* New York: 1904.

Cadwallader, Allen and David Gagne. *Analysis of Tonal Music: A Schenkerian Approach.* New York: University of Oxford Press, 2011.

Cruz, Francisco López. *Método para la enseñanza del cuatro puertorriqueño (Twelfth Edition).* San Juan: PR: Fundación Francisco López Cruz, 2012.

Deva, Dharma. "Musical Transculturation and Acculturation." http://www.rawa.asia/ethno/MUSICAL%20TRANSCULTURATION%20AND%20ACCULTURATION%20ESSAY.htm. 2000. Accessed October 25, 2015.

Duarte Loza, Daniel Martin. "Una poética pampa. Integración cultural entre Brasil, Argentina y Uruguay: música, clima, historia, y Geografía." *AURA. Revista de Historia y Teoría del Arte* No. 3 (2015). 17-37.

Duff, Ernest A. "Transculturation in Puerto Rico: The Reality of an American Cultural Imperialism." *Caribbean Affairs, Vol. 2, No. 1* (1989), 116-128.

Escabi, Pedro C. y Elsa M. Escabi. *La décima: Vista parcial del folklore.* Rio Piedras, PR: Editorial Universitaria. Universidad de Puerto Rico, 1976.

Fraga, Enrique. *La prohibición del lunfardo en la radiodifusión.* Argentina: Lajouane, 2006.

Frigerio, Alejandro "El Candombe Argentino: Crónica de una muerte anunciada." *Revista de Investigaciones Folklóricas* No. 8 (1993), 50-60.

García de León, Antonio. *El mar de los deseos: El Caribe hispano musical, Historia y contrapunto.* México: Siglo Veintiuno Editores, 2002.

González, José Luis. *Puerto Rico: El país de cuatro pisos y otros ensayos.* Rio Piedras, PR: Ediciones Huracán, 1987.

Gottschalk, Louis Moreau. *Souvenir de Porto Rico: Marche des Gibaros.* IMSLP Petrucci. http://petrucci.mus.auth.gr/imglnks/usimg/0/08/IMSLP121790-SIBLEY1802.6864.7db0-39087012347029_Souvenir_P.pdf. Accessed February 12, 2018.

Gross, Joan. "'Defendiendo la (Agri)Cultura: Reterritorializing Culture in the Puerto Rican Décima." *Oral Tradition* 23, Iss. 2 (2008). 219-234.

Haas, William H. "The Jibaro, an American Citizen." *Scientific Monthly* 43, No. 1 (1936), 33-46. http://jstor.org/stable/16218. Accessed June 6, 2016).

Hernández, José. *El gaucho Martin Fierro*. Buenos Aires: Imprenta de La Pampa. 1872. https://freeditorial.com/es/books/el-gaucho-martin-fierro. Accessed February 12, 2018. Public Domain.

Isolabella, Matías N. "Estructuras de improvisación en la payada rioplatense: definición y análisis." *Revista Argentina de Musicología* 12-13 (2012). 151-182.

Kartomi, Margaret J. "Los procesos y resultados del contacto cultural de la música: una discusión sobre la terminología y conceptos." *Etnomusicología* 25, No. 2 (1981). 227-249. http://www.jstor.org/stable/851273. Acceso el 20 de julio de 2016.

Lugones, Leopoldo. *El payador*. Buenos Aires: Oteri & Co. 1916.

Manuel Álvarez, Luis. "La décima en Puerto Rico como símbolo de identidad nacional." Valledupar, CO: *Foro Internacional sobre la Decima*. 2001. Conferencia. http://musica.uprrp.edu/lalvarez/seiseshtm/decima.htm. Accessed September 2, 2017.

Manuel, Peter. "Puerto Rican Music and Cultural Identity: Creative Appropriation of Cuban Sources from Danza to Salsa." *Etnomusicology* 38, No. 2 (1994). http://www.jstor.org/stable/851740. Accessed December 14, 2014.

Mason, J. Alden y Aurelio M. Espinosa. "Porto-Rican Folk-Lore. Décimas, Christmas Carols, Nursery Rhymes, and Other Songs." *Journal of American Folklore* 31, No. 121 (1918). http://www.jstor.org/stable/534783. Accessed January 19, 2018.

Nettl, Bruno. *The Study of Ethnomusicology: Thirty-Three Discussions*. Carbona, IL: University of Illinois Press, 2015.

Ortíz, Fernando. *Cuban Counterpoint, Tobacco and Sugar*. Translated by Harriet de Onis. New York: Alfred A. Knopf, 1947.

Pérez, Juan Sotomayor William Cumpiano y Myriam Fuentes. *Cuerdas de mi tierra: Una historia de los instrumentos de cuerda nativos de Puerto Rico: cuatro, tiple, vihuela y bordonúa* Naguabo, PR: Extreme Graphics, 2013.

Pooson, Sylvain. "*Entre Tango y Payada*: The Expression of Blacks in Argentina in the Nineteenth Century." *Confluencia* 20, No. 1 (2004). 87-99.

Posada, Consuelo. "La décima cantada en el Caribe y la fuerza de los procesos de identidad." *Revista de Literaturas Populares,* 3, No. 2 (2003). 141-154. Accessed January 19, 2018.

Ramos Samuel. *Los aguinaldos y seises para el cuatro puertorriqueño* (in Spanish and English). Samuel Ramos, 2012.

___. *Método de cuatro puertorriqueño, Vol. 1*. Samuel Ramos, 2011.

Romanuik, Ana María. "Hacia la búsqueda de la particularidad de 'modelo de hacer' de la música y los músicos pampeanos." *Sociedad Argentina para las Ciencias Cognitivas de la Música (SACCoM)*. 2011.

Rosa-Nieves, Cesáreo "Los Bailes de Puerto Rico." *Revista del Instituto de Cultura Puertorriqueña* No. 65, 1974, 14-18.

Santana, Déborah Berman. "Puerto Rico's Operation Bootstrap: Colonial Roots of a Persistent Model for 'Third World' Development" *Revista Geográfica, 124* (1998), bajo "JSTOR." http://www.jstor.org/stable/40992748. Accessed October 30, 2016.

Scarano, Francisco A. "La mascarada del jíbaro y la política subalterna de la formación de la identidad criolla en Puerto Rico, 1745-1823." *Revista de la historia americana* 101, No. 5 (1996), 1398-1431. http://www.jstor.org/stable/2170177. Accessed June 6, 2016.

Selser, Gregorio. "Prohíbese el tango 'Cambalache,' escrito en 1935. Molesto espejo." *El Dia*, October 26, 1981, 55.

Sixel, Friedrich W. "Inconsistencies in Transculturation Process." *Sociologus, Neue Folge/New Series* 19, No. 2 (1969), 166-177. http://www.jstor.org/stable/43644408. Accessed June 6, 2016.

Spottswood, Richard K. *Ethnic Music on Records: A Discography of Ethnic Rcordings Produced in the United States: 1893-1942—Volume 4: Spanish, Portuguese, Filipino, Basque*. Urbana, IL: University of Illinois Press, 1990.

Taylor, Diana. "Transculturating Transculturation." *Performing Arts Journal* 13, No. 2 (May 1991), under "JSTOR." http://www.jstor.org/stable/3245476. Accessed September 21, 2015.

___. *The Archive and the Repertoire: Performing Cultural Memory in the Americas*. Durham, NC: Imprenta de La Universidad de Duke, 2003.

Tomás, Navarro Tomás. *Métrica española: Reseña histórica y descriptiva* (Madrid: Ediciones Guadarrama, 1972), 268-269.

Torres-Robles, Carmen L. "La mitificación y demitificación del jíbaro como símbolo de la identidad nacional puertorriqueña." *Bilingual Review/ Revista Bilingüe* 24, No. 3 (1999), 241-253. http://www.jstor.org/stable/25745665. Accessed June 6, 2016.

Viala, Fabienne. *The Post-Columbus Syndrome: Identities, Cultural Nationalism, and Commemorations in the Caribbean*. New York: Palgrave Macmillan, 2014.

Vidal, Paloma y Claudia Púa Reyes, *La armonía en el tango. Un estudio desde el análisis armónico.*" Santiago, CL: Universidad de Chile, 2010, 17. Seminario de Título Profesor Especializado en Teoría General de la Música.

Webography

Bertazza, Juan Pablo. "Si se calla el cantor," *Página 12*. https://www.pagina12.com.ar/diario/suplementos/radar/9-4990-2008-12-14.html. Accessed April 18, 2018.

Chuliver, Raúl. "El gaucho en la historia y en la tradición argentina," (Buenos Aires: Premio Santa Clara de Asis, 2015). *Biblioteca virtual Miguel de Cervantes.* http://www.cervantesvirtual.com/obra-visor/el-gaucho-en-la-historia-y-en-la-tradicion-argentina-784360/html/. Accessed March 10, 2018.

Conservatorio de Artes del Caribe. "Los estilos musicales folklóricos de Puerto Rico." 2014. http://www.artesdelcaribe.com/los-estilos-musicales-folkloricos-de-puerto-rico/. Accessed January 28, 2018.

Constitución de la Nación Argentina Completa con los Tratados de Jerarqui Constitucional. Buenos Aires: Biblioteca Virtual Universal, 2017. http://www.biblioteca.org.ar/libros/201250.pdf. Accessed February 12, 2018.

Davila, Virgilio. "El jíbaro." Poem Hunter, https://www.poemhunter.com/poem/el-j-baro/comments/. Accesed March 3, 2018.

De Bassi, Antonio y Manuel Romero. "Ignacio Corsini- El adiós de Gabino Ezeiza- Milonga." https://www.youtube.com/watch?v=scIMM3TW8E0. Accessed February 8, 2018.

Decimania. "La Semana del Trovador Puertorriqueño." http://www.decimania.com/index.php/semana-del-trovador. Accessed April 10, 2018.

"Encuentro Santosvegano de Payadores de San Clemente 2017." *Televisión Pública Argentina,* http://www.tvpublica.com.ar/programa/36-encuentro-santosvegano-de-payadores-de-san-clemente-2017/. Accessed April 9, 2018.

Ezeiza, Gabino. "Gabino Ezeiza & Guitarra- El Tango Patagones-1905." https://www.youtube.com/watch?v=dOchX98rVnY&index=1&list=LL8mqJY4bOeb4IP285vKj4OA&t=0s. Accessed February 8, 2018.

Folklore Tradiciones. "Payadores—La Payada." 2004-2016. https://www.folkloretradiciones.com.ar/payadores1.htm#L. Accessed January 22, 2018.

González, Yair/Bennú. "Podcast Payada." *Soundcloud* (2017). https://soundcloud.com/jazzyzoe/podcast-payada. Accessed January 24, 2018.

"HD Programa 017- Temporada 8- Afroargentinos." (2013). https://www.youtube.com/watch?v=eUik0wa96HY&list=LL8mqJY4bOeb4IP285vKj4OA&index=2. Accessed February 8, 2018.

Historiador Argentino. *Argentina: cultura gaucha*, https://www.youtube.com/watch?v=eESgmILx4Y4&list=LL8mqJY4bOeb4IP285vKj4OA&index=3&t=0s. Accessed February 8, 2018.

Jara, Fernanda. "Cumple 100 años "Mi noche triste", el primer tango canción grabado por Gardel." *Infobae*. https://www.infobae.com/cultura/2017/06/11/cumple-100-anos-mi-noche-triste-el-primer-tango-cancion-grabado-por-gardel/. Accessed April 13, 2018.

"Luis Manuel Álvarez explica la evolución de la música en Puerto Rico" (Extracto del documental *Salsa Opus 3* por Yves Billón de 1991, traducción en inglés), https://www.youtube.com/watch?v=EJ0RmsuKFHY&index=6&list=LL8mqJY4bOeb4IP285vKj4OA&t=0s (accessed February 8, 2018).

Mdz. "Historia cronológica de la radio en Argentina." https://www.mdzol.com/nota/232937-historia-cronologica-de-la-radio-en-la-argentina/. Accessed March 12, 2018.

Morales, David. "Grabaciones tempranas de música jíbara puertorriqueña: 1909-1910." *La Clave* (Blog), http://plenama.blogspot.com/2011/06/early-audio-recordings-of-puerto-rican.html?m=1. Accessed March 14, 2018.

Mundo Sur 106.5. "Historia de la radio en Argentina." http://www.mundosurfm.com/historia-de-la-radio-en-la-argentina/. Accessed March 12, 2018.

"Noticias: Locales: Frases peculiares de la cultura boricua." *El nuevo día*, martes, el 26 de noviembre de 2013. https://www.elnuevodia.com/noticias/locales/nota/frasespeculiaresdelaculturaboricua-1652910/. Accessed March 10, 2018.

Observador, El: "Mi noche triste." "Cien anos atrás, Gardel estrenaba el primer tango canción de la historia," *Perfil,* el 7 de enero de 2017. http://www.perfil.com/elobservador/cien-anos-atras-gardel-estrenaba-el-primer-tango-cancion-de-la-historia.phtml. Accessed April 13, 2018.

Orquesta de San Sebastián. "Seis Tango." https://www.youtube.com/watch?v=4rYYWjOXO1g. Accessed February 8, 2018.

"Payada del campo argentino." https://www.youtube.com/watch?v=DaifV8QFUb0&t=117s. Accessed March 13, 2018.

Payadas, "Santos Vega El alma del payador," http://payadas.com/santos-vega-el-alma-de-payador. Accessed March 5, 2018).

Proyecto del Cuatro Puertorriqueño. "Decimas inspiradas por el cuatro puertorriqueño." http://www.cuatro-pr.org/es/node/171. Accessed March 5, 2018.

___. "Nuestra Música Campesina: El Seis." http://www.cuatro-pr.org/es/node/179. Accessed January 23, 2018.

___. "Nuestra Música Campesina: La Decima Puertorriqueña." http://www.cuatro-pr.org/es/node/97. Accessed January 23, 2018.

___. "Nuestra Música Campesina: Muestra de 36 Distintos Seises y Aguinaldos." http://www.cuatro-pr.org/es/node/186. Accessed January 23, 2018.

Rodri, Jann. "Puerto Rico se levanta seis pampero (cosas buenas sacaré)," https://www.youtube.com/watch?v=VvpNZk43Ghw. Accessed February 8, 2018.

Roper, Jonathan. "'Our National Folklore': William Thoms as Cultural Nationalist." In *Narrating the (Trans) Nation: The Dialects of Culture and Identity*. Edited by Krishna Sen and Sudeshna Chakravari (Calcutta, ID: Das Gupta & Co., 2008), 60-74. https://www.academia.edu/835266/_Our_National_Folklore_William_Thoms_as_Cultural_Nationalist. Accessed March 10, 2018.

Saborboricuapr1. "Seis Milonga Instrumental (Cuatro Puertorriqueño)." https://www.youtube.com/watch?v=2KiavRgeV80. Accessed April 16, 2018.

Sanchez, Anthony Luis. *The Puerto Rican Cuatro as a Device for Transculturation: A Contemporary Compositional Approach in Estampas de La Isla del Encanto*. Athens, GA: University of Georgia, 2017. DMA Dissertation. http://dbs.galib.uga.edu/cgi-bin/getd.cgi?userid=galileo&serverno=22&instcode=publ. Accessed November 27, 2018.

Tinta Digital PR. "Comienzos de la radio en Puerto Rico," http://tintadigitalpr.com/blog/comienzos-de-la-radio-en-puerto-rico/. Accessed March 12, 2018.

Torres, Jaime Torres. "Roberto Silva, nuevo trovador nacional." *Fundación Nacional para la Cultura Popular*, el 20 de noviembre de 2015. https://prpop.org/2015/11/roberto-silva-nuevo-trovador-nacional/. Accessed April 10, 2018.

Torres, Luis Llorens. "Trova gaucha." *Proyecto salón de hogar*, el 19 de abril de 2010. http://www.proyectosalonhogar.com/escritores/Poesia_puertorriquena.htm#llorens. Accessed March 10, 2018.

Very Tango Store. "La historia de la milonga." https://www.verytangostore.com/tango-milonga.html. Accessed February 12, 2018.

<u>Discography</u>

Discépolo, Enrique Santos. "Cambalache," *Enrique Santos Discépolo: "Poet of the Tango"—Bs As Tango*. Buenos Aires (¿?): El Bandoneón, 2010.

Gaeta, Luis (Narrator) y London Symphony Orchestra (Gisele Ben-Dor), *Ginastera: Estancia- Panambi*. Naxos, 2006. Spotify.

"Nothing is impossible for those who try."
-Alexander, the Great

www.ingramcontent.com/pod-product-compliance
Lightning Source LLC
Chambersburg PA
CBHW070435010526
44118CB00014B/2049